The Deserted and The Dancing Girl's Daughter

An abridged English version of the Silappatikāram and the Maṇimēkalai

S. Sriskandarajah
&
Robin McGlashan

Grosvenor House Publishing Limited

This book is published by
Grosvenor House Publishing Ltd
28-30 High Street, Guildford, Surrey, GU1 3HY.
www.grosvenorhousepublishing.co.uk

A CIP record for this book
is available from the British Library

ISBN 978-1-908105-10-3

CONTENTS

PREFACE

In this volume, we have brought together the two earliest Tamil epic poems, which were composed perhaps as early as the second century CE. They are known in Tamil as the Silappatikāram, which means the story of the anklet, and the Maṇimēkalai, which is the personal name of the heroine. We have taken the liberty of giving to the poems English names that reflect the characteristics of their two heroines, "The deserted wife" and "The dancing girl's daughter".

These two poems have traditionally been known as "the twin epics" because the Maṇimēkalai follows the Silappatikāram as its sequel. In this abridged version, the story of the Maṇimēkalai presupposes that the reader is familiar with all that happened previously in the Silappatikāram. Maṇimēkalai, the heroine of the second poem which bears her name, is the daughter of Mātavi, who plays a major role in the Silappatikāram as a courtesan, a professional musician and dancer. So, although the two poems are very different in other ways, they are rightly seen as belonging together.

For the benefit of readers who are not familiar with the story, we have included in an appendix a key to all the proper names and non-English words that occcur in these poems. Guides to the system of transliteration used and to the pronunciation of Tamil words are also given in appendices.

As authors of this version, we have long enjoyed these stories in their simple beauty and poetry and in their drama and pathos, and we would like to share that pleasure with a new generation of readers. At the same time, we are aware that much captivating colour and detail is lost in this brief retelling of the tales.

Nevertheless, although readers are given here only a bare outline, it is our hope that those who lack, and may never attain, the advanced level of Tamil knowledge necessary to read these epics in the original, will enjoy the stories for their own sake, and so be encouraged to explore in the future more of the rich treasury of Tamil literature that is available in English translation.

In fact, the present work is part of a long-standing endeavour on our part to bring to a wider readership something of the rich and ancient literary heritage of the Tamil people. That heritage spans more than two thousand years, but still remains largely unrecognized in the wider world. Earlier contributions which the two of us have made to this endeavour independently include such books as "Ethical essence of the Tamils" (1993), "The history of the holy servants of the Lord Siva" (2006), "Scenes from Tamil classics" (2009) and "Tiruttoṇṭar Tiruvantāti" (2009).

In this connection, we would like to extend our thanks to Dr Avvai Natarajan of Chennai, Tamil Nadu, one time Vice-Chancellor of the Tamil University, Tanjore. He has consistently encouraged the production of books in English on Tamil culture and literature.

We would also like to express our gratitude to Mrs Shobana Janakan MSc for her willing and skilled cooperation in preparing the text of this book for the publishers.

Finally, we are grateful to Grosvenor House Publications for their kind and efficient cooperation throughout the process of producing this book, and for the excellent quality of the end-product of their work.

INTRODUCTION

The Silappatikāram and the Maṇimēkalai are very long poems, or collections of poems, written many centuries ago. They were written in a land and among a people that were very different from anything that we know today. They tell the story of ordinary men and women who lived in those times and in that land. Because their background is so different from ours, this brief Introduction has been included to try to help the reader make sense of the two stories.

Both poems are love stories, but with a great deal of religious content. The Silappatikāram is a story about an unfaithful husband, Kōvalaṉ, who deserts his virtuous wife, Kaṇṇaki, and sets up house with the courtesan Mātavi. When he tires of her and returns to Kaṇṇaki, his attempt to rebuild his life leads to his own death and the destruction of a great city. Because Kaṇṇaki is the heroine of this poem, we have given it the English title "The deserted wife".

The Maṇimēkalai, which takes its name from its heroine, is a continuation of the story of the Silappatikāram. The girl Maṇimēkalai is the daughter of Kōvalaṉ and Mātavi, born out of wedlock. Hence our English title, "The dancing girl's daughter". Maṇimēkalai is pursued by the Chōḻa prince, Utayakumaraṉ, and her efforts to escape his attentions lead to many adventures. Finally the prince is murdered as the result of a misunderstanding, and Maṇimēkalai herself becomes a Buddhist nun.

As the Silappatikāram itself tells us at the very beginning, in those days there were three important kingdoms in South India where the Tamil people lived. One was the land ruled by the kings of the Chōḻa dynasty. This land lay in the plains on either side of the river Kāviri, and in the delta region of that river where it flows into the Bay of Bengal. Its capital was the port city of Kāvirippūm Paṭṭiṉam, also known as Pūmpukār.

A second kingdom, to the South of the Chōḻa country, was ruled by kings of the Pāṇḍiya dynasty. It was bounded by the sea on the East, and by the mountains of the Western Ghats on the West. It stretched as far South as Cape Comorin, the very southernmost tip of India. Its capital was the city of Maturai, on the banks of the Vaikai river.

The third kingdom was ruled by the Chēra kings, who had their capital at Vañchi. Their kingdom lay to the West of the other two kingdoms. It included the mountainous region of the Western Ghats and the Western sea coast of India, which is now included in the state of Kerala.

The story told in the Silappatikāram takes place in each of those kingdoms, one after the other, beginning in the Chōḻa country, then moving to the Pāṇḍiya country, and ending in the Chēra country. The poem is in fact divided into three parts, each one named after the capital city of the Tamil kingdom in which the action of that part is primarily set. The action of the Maṇimēkalai mainly takes place in the Chōḻa capital, Pūmpukār, but also extends to islands across the sea.

At the time when these stories took place, as at the later period when the stories were written down, the Tamil people were not all Hindus. Many of them were Jains, and many others Buddhists. In the Silappatikāram, members of these three religions seem to have lived together happily side by side, and a major role is played by a sage of the Jain religion.

In the Maṇimēkalai there seems to be more of an atmosphere of conflict between the religions, and one in particular is favoured more than the others. The original version of this story includes long religious discourses setting out the teachings of Buddhism, and the heroine herself and her mother finally accept that religion.

In those days, women held a very different place in Tamil society from what we see today. Whereas women were expected to be faithful to a single husband, men held a dominant position in society and were free from any such restraints.

There was one particular group of women known as "courtesans". They were trained to a high standard in music and dance, and earned their living by giving their company and their favours to wealthy men in return for money. Mātavi, who plays a major role in the story of the Silappatikāram, was one of these women.

The present version is not a complete translation of these two epic poems. Many of the songs and poems included in the Silappatikāram and the religious discourses in the Maṇimēkalai have been left out, because they do not directly contribute to the unfolding of the story.

Rather, we have tried to give the reader an abridged version of the poems in simple English prose, which keeps the story moving while preserving as far as possible the character of the original. If the reader feels the need for further background information before plunging into the story, it may be found in the Epilogue at the end. Otherwise, read on ....

THE DESERTED WIFE

Part I - Pūmpukār

1

The marriage of Kaṇṇaki and Kōvalaṉ

In ancient times, the Tamil people were ruled by three dynasties of kings, the Chēra dynasty, the Chōḻa dynasty, and the Pāṇḍiya dynasty. The capital of the Chōḻa country was Kāvirippūm Paṭṭiṉam, also known as Pūmpukār. The city got its name because it was situated at the mouth of the river Kāviri. It was renowned for the wealth of its merchants and the splendour of the mansions in which they lived.

In Kāvirippūm Paṭṭiṉam there lived a merchant of fabulous wealth called Mānāykaṉ, who had a beautiful daughter called Kaṇṇaki. When the girl reached twelve years of age, according to the custom of those days, her father decided to look for a suitable husband for her. Hundreds of horoscopes were studied and compared.

Eventually, the horoscope of Kōvalaṉ, the son of another merchant of Kāvirippūm Paṭṭiṉam called Māsāttuvāṉ, was found to match the horoscope of Kaṇṇaki. So after several weeks of detailed, practical negotiations, the elders of the two families decided that the marriage of Kōvalaṉ and Kaṇṇaki should go ahead.

In that city, Kaṇṇaki was famed for her surpassing beauty and the sweetness of her character. Kōvalaṉ was renowned for his business skill and generosity. As Mānāykaṉ and Māsāttuvāṉ were men of great wealth and reputation, plans were made for a magnificent wedding to be held at an auspicious time on an auspicious day. For many days the wedding of Kōvalaṉ and Kaṇṇaki was the talk of the town.

After their marriage had taken place, the two young people lived happily together in their own separate house, free from any interference from their parents. Kōvalaṉ was liked and admired by all, while Kaṇṇaki's devotion to her husband won his ever increasing affection.

As the years passed, their life together continued like an unending honey-moon. Although the couple wished to have a baby to seal their married love, they were denied that happiness. When they consulted astrologers about the situation, it was predicted that there would be a long delay, but they should not give up hope. This prolonged delay did not diminish their love and affection for each other one bit. Meanwhile Kaṇṇaki's household duties and Kōvalaṉ's business activities kept the two of them fully occupied.

2

Kōvalaṉ deserts Kaṇṇaki

Kāvirippūm Paṭṭiṉam was a busy commercial town which was buzzing with activity day and night. It had a big harbour where ships were constantly coming and going. Merchants from Rome, Greece, Arabia, and Lanka all had their own quarters in the city where they carried on their trade. So all sorts of people from many different backgrounds and countries lived and worked together there.

Among the people who lived and plied their trade in that city, there was a courtesan named Chitrāpati. She had a daughter called Mātavi, who was a beautiful girl highly accomplished in classical Tamil dance and music.

Mātavi had started to learn these arts at the age of five, and by the time that she was twelve she had mastered all their finer points. Because Chitrāpati was an ambitious lady, she wanted her daughter to make a mark in life. As a noted courtesan and performer herself, Chitrāpati was very famous and even had connections with the royal court. So she planned for Mātavi's first public performance to take place in the royal presence and under the patronage of the king.

Mātavi's debut

When Chitrāpati approached the palace officials and made known her desire, the king graciously granted her request. So the day was fixed and magnificent arrangements were made for Mātavi's first public performance.

Since Mātavi wanted her performance to be judged by the best performers of the day, invitations were sent to all the famous dancers and musicians of the land. A stage was set up which was beautifully lit and decorated, and the very best orchestra of the time was engaged. The fragrance from the flower garlands hanging on either side of the stage filled the hall and created the ideal mood for Mātavi's first concert.

At the auspicious hour, Mātavi came onto the stage. Placing her right foot forward, she first leant against the pillar on the right hand side of the stage. Ceremonial music from the orchestra filled the hall. Then as the music faded, Mātavi took centre stage. She danced like Mēṉakai, the celestial dancer, to the accompaniment of the *mirutaṅkam*, the flute and *the yāḻ.* The audience were mesmerised by her artistry, and watched her performance spell bound.

The king, who was himself a connoisseur of music and dance, was delighted. He congratulated Mātavi and presented her with bars of pure gold worth a fortune. In addition he personally decorated Mātavi with the royal medal called "*talaikkōl*", and gave her a priceless gold chain set with emeralds. Chitrāpati felt on top of the world, and Mātavi's happiness knew no bounds.

Although Mātavi was still of tender age, according to the old tradition of the courtesan class, Chitrāpati wanted to take advantage of the great occasion of her first concert to make her daughter become the companion of some wealthy person in the city. The other members of Chitrāpati's family gave their approval to this plan.

Kōvalaṉ buys the chain

Accordingly, Chitrāpati handed the gold chain set with emeralds to her servant Kūṉi, and told her to take her stand at a vantage point on the main bazaar road of the city. There she was to announce that Mātavi, the famous dancer, would become the courtesan of any man who could buy the priceless chain of gold and emeralds.

That chain was so valuable that no one was able to raise the money to buy it and so make Mātavi their property. The news that Mātavi was on sale in the market place, with details about the asking price, reached the ears of Kōvalaṉ who was busy at the other end of the city. Now Kōvalaṉ was a musician himself, and a lover of art and music. He had already heard of Mātavi's beauty and talent. So when the news reached him that she was on offer, he took the number of gold coins required and rushed to the bazaar.

Chitrāpati's servant maid, Kūṉi, was at her post surrounded by young business men who were longing to buy the services of Mātavi, but had not enough money to do so. It was growing dark and the chances of finding a buyer were fading. Kūṉi was growing anxious that she might fail to find anyone who could buy the emerald chain and so become the lord of Mātavi.

As the sun was sinking down towards the western horizon in a deep red glow, Kōvalaṉ reached the spot where Kūṉi was announcing the sale. Without a moment's hesitation he paid the purchase price in gold, and followed Kūṉi to Mātavi's house. There Chitrāpati was waiting eagerly for Kūṉi's return with a buyer. As Kūṉi entered the house, Kōvalaṉ followed behind with a guilty conscience.

3

Kōvalan̠'s new life of pleasure

Chitrāpati and Mātavi were shocked, and at the same time pleasantly surprised, to see Kōvalan̠ the great merchant of Kāvirippūm Paṭṭin̠am on their doorstep. They knew that Kōvalan̠ belonged to a family of noble merchants famous for their upright behaviour. Although Chitrāpati was worried in her heart of hearts, she was happy too that Mātavi was lucky enough to become the courtesan to a man from Māsāttuvān̠'s family.

As for Mātavi, glancing sidelong at Kōvalan̠, she felt both shy and fearful. Kōvalan̠ could not take his eyes from the beautiful girl. When their eyes met, their hearts were knit together as one. Kōvalan̠ forgot that he was already married. Mātavi could not acknowledge that Kōvalan̠ belonged to another woman. All thought of Kaṇṇaki vanished from Kōvalan̠'s mind. He was bewitched by Mātavi and could not let her out of his sight.

The news that Chitrāpati had managed to secure Kōvalan̠ for Mātavi spread like wild fire. It reached the ears of Kaṇṇaki and her parents. The families of Mānāykaṉ and Māsāttuvāṉ hung their heads in shame when Kōvalaṉ's action became the talk of the town, but they realised that there was nothing that they could do.

Kaṇṇaki’s reaction to her loss

Kaṇṇaki's life became empty and hollow overnight. She had believed that Kōvalaṉ loved her dearly, and she had never given him any cause for complaint. She never imagined that all of a sudden he would act in a manner so foreign to his character.

Kaṇṇaki's companion, Tēvanti, offered to seek the help of some wise older folk, to try to bring Kōvalaṉ back. But, fearing that such a move might offend Kōvalaṉ further, Kaṇṇaki turned her offer down.

Though Kaṇṇaki was very young in age, the way she had been brought up had given her a wisdom beyond her years. Her parents knew their daughter well, so they did not interfere when her husband deserted her. Meanwhile Kōvalaṉ began a new life with Mātavi, enjoying what his money had bought.

Although women like Chitrāpati played an important part in the life of the Chōḻa country, they were regarded as second class citizens among the ancient Tamil people. Mātavi was like a lotus flower born in the mud. She was upright, chaste and honest. But she was barely twelve years old when Kōvalaṉ decided to take her as his companion.

Kōvalan̲ and Mātavi's life together

At that time Mātavi hardly had a will or a mind of her own. She simply did what her mother told her, and her mother did not see anything wrong in giving Mātavi to a married man, provided that he could pay for the emerald chain given her by the Chōl̲a king. Nor did Mātavi see anything wrong in stealing the husband of another woman. However, from their first meeting Mātavi loved Kōvalan̲ from the bottom of her heart.

Kōvalan̲ also found many things in Mātavi for which he had been yearning during the years that he had spent with Kaṇṇaki. Kōvalan̲ was a skilled musician, who had mastered the ancient stringed instrument called the "*yāl̲*". Since Kaṇṇaki was a simple woman who had no taste for art or music, Kōvalan̲ could not cultivate his musical tastes during his years with her. But when he met Mātavi, Kōvalan̲ had the opportunity to revive his interest in music. So he simply fell for Mātavi and forgot Kaṇṇaki, despite all her charms.

The main reason for the love that blossomed between Kōvalan̲ and Mātavi was music. True, she was beautiful too, but she had trained to perfection in music, dance and make-up. In short, she was a girl of many talents, who met all Kōvalan̲'s needs in every way imaginable. Their life together was a bed of roses. Since Kōvalan̲ was endowed with great wealth from his business activities, they did not go short of material comforts either.

4

Kōvalaṉ picks a quarrel

As the years rolled on happily for Mātavi, there was no let up in the tears that rolled down Kaṇṇaki's cheeks. However, in his blind love for Mātavi, Kōvalaṉ failed to give proper attention to the business interests which he had inherited from his father. Instead, he spent most of his time with Mātavi, totally absorbed in the leisure pursuits which they shared. As a result, his business, and with it his wealth, began to be badly affected.

Although Mātavi loved Kōvalaṉ and could even be said to have been a more suitable wife for him than Kaṇṇaki, she failed in her duty to look after their household affairs. Although some blame must attach to Kōvalaṉ also, she lived like a spend-thrift, who believed that there was no limit to his wealth.

Almost five years after he and Mātavi started to live together as husband and wife, they were blessed with a daughter. Kōvalaṉ named the child Maṇimēkalai after the deity who was traditionally believed to have rescued one of Kōvalaṉ's ancestors.

Mātavi and Kōvalaṉ held a great naming ceremony for their daughter, and he gave valuable presents to all who attended. His aim was to give help whenever and wherever it was possible. His generosity and Mātavi's exemplary life made the people of Kāvirippūm Paṭṭiṉam pardon their failings. Together they rode the crest of a wave of fame and popularity.

The festival of Indra

Since the city was a place where people of many nations met, it never slept, but was always buzzing with colourful festivities. One such event was the ancient festival of Indra, the Lord of the heavens and god of the fertile farmlands. This festival was held in the month of Chittirai (April) under the patronage of the Chōḻa king in his capital city of Kāvirippūm Paṭṭiṉam. It lasted for twenty-eight days, and ended on the day of the full moon in that month.

The festivities of the Indra festival were held in the bazaar and on the beach, and continued round the clock. It was an occasion for everyone to meet, to feast and to join in the revels.

Since it was the season for music and dance heralding the coming of spring, skilled members of the courtesan class attracted the attention of all eyes. Mātavi was booked to give dance peformances and musical recitals at several places around the city. Kōvalaṉ willingly allowed her to take part in those events, since they gave her deep pleasure and also won her fame.

On the final day of the festival, after Mātavi had given pleasure to the music lovers of Kāvirippūm Paṭṭin̲am in the morning, she and Kōvalan̲ decided to keep the evening free for themselves. They wanted to enjoy the evening time on the moonlit shore of the city.

So they put on colourful clothes and set out for the beach. It was crowded with people, including all kinds of merchants and traders who had already set out their stalls. They were busy selling jewelry, perfume, wine, food stuffs and snacks.

Mātavi and Kōvalan̲ chose a place under the shade of a laurel tree, where their attendants put up a comfortable shelter and decorated it with beautiful paintings. There without a care they sat and watched the young people having fun around them.

Suspicion creeps in

As Kōvalan̲ and Mātavi whiled away the time talking about this and that, a maid of Mātavi brought her mistress's *yāl̲* and put it in front of her. As if she had been waiting for it, Mātavi picked it up, tuned it, and handing it to Kōvalan̲, looked into his eyes expectantly. Kōvalan̲ gladly took the *yāl̲*, and as he touched the strings, he began to create the mood in which he wanted to play. Although he was in a cheerful mood, he recalled that the sweetest songs are those that give voice to the saddest thoughts. So he began to sing in a sombre and sorrowful mode.

Kōvalaṉ composed the words of his song on the spur of the moment. They conveyed the lonely feelings of a young lover longing to rejoin his beloved whom he had not seen for a long time. However, the feelings evoked by his singing were so real and natural that, although Mātavi had never doubted that Kōvalaṉ was faithful to her, her faith in him now began to waver, and suspicion reared its ugly head. Without allowing her suspicions to show in her face, she took back the *yāḻ* from him and retuned it to suit her own pitch.

When she had set the appropriate mood, Mātavi began to sing. She too chose a sad mode, composing her own words as she sang. She chose the same theme as Kōvalaṉ, and sang a song that reflected the sadness of a girl separated from her lover and longing for reunion.

In Mātavi's song, there was deeper feeling and more pain than in Kōvalaṉ's, so that he was totally captivated by it. It was only when Mātavi had finished singing that he realised what it was that she was singing about. Then the devil of suspicion overpowered him, and the thought that after all Mātavi belonged to a class of base women who sold their bodies for a price, came back again and again to torment him.

Mātavi sang as she did partly as a joke, to pay him back for his song. On the other hand, without good reason and quite against his own experience of her, Kōvalaṉ thought that Mātavi must be having a secret affair. Unbeknown to him, she must have a secret lover, he concluded, and it was about him that she now sang with such longing.

Kōvalan̲'s rash conclusion

Kōvalan̲ stood up abruptly, and left the place without a word. Mātavi and her servant Vasantamālai were aghast. They were at a loss to know what had happened. Worried and helpless, Mātavi packed up her things and left for home. She hoped that that was where Kōvalan̲ had gone, and that she could pacify him when they met again.

However, when Mātavi reached home, Kōvalan̲ was nowhere to be seen. It then dawned on her that she must have really offended him. She could not guess where he had gone, although she still had hopes that he would come back sooner rather than later. When she sent out her servants to look for him, they searched everywhere but returned empty handed.

Mātavi writes to Kōvalan̲

The next day, Mātavi decided to write a touching letter to Kōvalan̲, telling him of her love. She made a garland of champak, jasmine, and lily, plaited together with other flowers and leaves. On one of the broad leaves of the garland she wrote her letter, using the pointed end of a young flower bud as a pen and a mixture of *kuṅkumam* and other fragrant herbs as ink.

"This is the season when the god of the spring time brings together the male and the female of all kinds of living creatures," she wrote. "Every evening, the moon too stirs up passionate desires, while Kāmaṉ shoots his arrows into the hearts of lonely lovers. Please try to understand my pain.”

Although she had no inkling of Kōvalaṉ’s whereabouts, Mātavi gave the garland containing her letter to Vasantamālai to deliver to him. The servant went to all the places which she knew to be his favourite haunts. When at last she found him in a busy shopping street, she was overwhelmed with joy. She rushed up to him and greeted him in the usual way.

Kōvalaṉ reacted coolly to her greeting and would not even speak to her. She respectfully stretched out her hand to give him Mātavi's garland, but he would not accept it. He shouted out that all dancers are clever and deceitful, and that he was no longer prepared to be taken in. With that, he turned on his heel and walked off.

Unable to deliver her letter, Vasantamālai returned to Mātavi disappointed, and told her all that had happened. Mātavi now realised that Kōvalaṉ was really angry, and she felt terrible. She regretted that her vanity and wish for revenge had caused this tragic misunderstanding.

For his part, Kōvalaṉ failed to realise that it was his song that had sowed the seeds for the ugly scene of the previous evening. He was embarrassed to face his parents, and equally reluctant to return to Kaṇṇaki, although in the recent past he had visited her house from time to time to collect jewels for Mātavi's use. He could not make up his mind whether to return to his parents' house or to Kaṇṇaki's.

After long soul searching, Kōvalaṉ decided to return to Kaṇṇaki in the hope that she would take him back, in spite of the way that he had treated her. So he set off in that direction.

5

Kaṇṇaki and Kōvalaṉ leave Pūmpukār

From the time that Kōvalaṉ had deserted her and started to enjoy the pleasures of Mātavi's company, Kaṇṇaki was pining for him, and hoping against hope that one day he would return to her. However, she never spoke a word of criticism against him, although some of her relations and friends begged her to confront him and to urge him to return to his lawful wedded wife.

The houses where Kaṇṇaki and Mātavi lived were only a few miles apart. But, although Pūmpukār was full of gossip and rumour, what happened at Mātavi's house never reached the ears of Kaṇṇaki.

Years had rolled by, and Kaṇṇaki's routine remained unchanged, except that she could no longer serve her husband or be of help to Brahmins and wandering holy men. Her only comfort during the time of separation was that she could still serve Kōvalaṉ's elderly parents. They loved and cared for her greatly, and did all that they could to soften the pain of her separation from Kōvalaṉ.

Kaṇṇaki was a practical person and did not have great faith in the old beliefs and rituals. But her friend Tēvanti firmly believed in all the old traditions and conventions. So she regularly visited the temple of Sāttaṉ and prayed for Kaṇṇaki's well being.

One day after Tēvanti had offered a special prayer at the temple, she went straight to the house of Kaṇṇaki with the *prasādam* which she had been given. She told Kaṇṇaki that during her worship at the temple she had prayed for her well-being and for her reunion with Kōvalaṉ. She added that she was confident that the Almighty would graciously relieve her loneliness. Kaṇṇaki did not share Tēvanti's confidence. Nevertheless she told Tēvanti that she hoped her words would come true.

Kaṇṇaki's dream

At that moment Kaṇṇaki was feeling deeply troubled by a bad dream which she had had the night before. "I had a terrible dream last night," she confided to Tēvanti. "Holding each other's hand, my huband and I went to a town the name of which I cannot now remember. There my husband was falsely accused of committing some crime. He was found guilty and punished by the king. I protested to the king, and threatened the city with dire consequences. I cannot tell you any more about it, but if you heard how it all ended, you would think me crazy."

At first Tēvanti was taken aback by the dream. When she had regained her composure, she said,

"Kaṇṇaki, you must always remember this: your husband did not hate you, but all these years for some mysterious reason he has put you out of his mind. Perhaps it was fate. Or perhaps this misery has come upon you because in a previous birth you failed to perform the proper fast which would ensure that you got a good husband. But there is a way to atone for such a failure.

"At the mouth of the river Kāviri, there are two holy places sacred to the sun and to the moon. Nearby there is a temple of Kāmaṉ, the god of love. Women who bathe in the river there and worship Kāmaṉ are sure to win back the husbands they have lost. If you would like to, one day we could visit those holy places."

Having listened patiently to what Tēvanti said with such good intentions, Kaṇṇaki replied, "It would not be right for me to do that. A married woman should worship no other deity but her husband."

Kōvalaṉ's return

While they were still talking, Kaṇṇaki's maid came in and announced that Kōvalaṉ was waiting at the gate. Kaṇṇaki could not believe her ears. She hurried to the gate, and true enough, there he was. "Come in, my lord," she said, and ushered him in.

Kōvalaṉ wept to see how thin Kaṇṇaki had become while he had been away. "Kaṇṇaki," he pleaded, "please forgive me! I have done you great wrong. I went after a dancing girl whose life is full of lies, and I have wasted all the wealth my forebears handed down to me. Now I have nothing left, and I am deeply ashamed."

At first Kaṇṇaki could not grasp what he was saying. She was not sure whether he had come back to her for good, or whether once again he had come to ask for more jewels. However, in truth Kaṇṇaki knew that she had nothing left to give him. Over the last few years, Kōvalan̲ had taken everything she had.

"All that I have left is a pair of jewelled anklets," Kaṇṇaki replied. "You are free to take them".

Kōvalan̲ was shocked by Kaṇṇaki's offer. For the first time in years, he clasped her hands and said, "No, Kaṇṇaki, no! I am now a changed man. I have come back to you for good. I will sell one of your anklets, and with the money that I get for it, I will take up again my trading business. In that way I will recover all that I have lost. The honour of my family, though, is in ruins. That I can never restore."

"Now I am so ashamed of what I have done," he went on, "I cannot live in Kāvirippūm Paṭṭin̲am any longer. Let us go to Maturai and start a new life there. Get ready at once, and we will leave the city without delay. No one shall know about it, neither friend nor foe, neither your parents nor mine. Tell Tēvanti and the servants to keep it a secret for a full week after we have gone."

Kaṇṇaki was dumbfounded. Mixed feelings welled up within her. She was happy that Kōvalan̲ realised how foolish he had been, and that he had now come back to her. However, it was difficult for her to accept the idea of leaving Kāvirippūm Paṭṭiṉam without speaking to her parents and parents-in-law, who had been so good to her all this time. It was equally difficult for her to say anything against the wishes of her husband, who had at last come back to her after years of separation.

That night they packed up whatever they could take, and in the small hours of the following morning they bade goodbye to Kāvirippūm Paṭṭiṉam with a heavy heart.

6

Mātavi tries to put things right

Mātavi meanwhile was quite unaware of the fact that Kōvalaṉ and Kaṇṇaki were now reconciled, and that together they had left for Maturai. She thought that Kōvalaṉ would need some time to come to his senses, but that he would certainly return to her on the following day. Although she tried to persuade herself that this would happen, she was distraught and spent the night sleepless, weeping into her pillow.

When the day dawned, there was no sign of Kōvalaṉ's return. As the sun rose high in the sky, news spread that Kōvalaṉ and Kaṇṇaki had left the city for an unknown destination. Even Mānāykaṉ's family knew nothing about it.

Vasantamālai went to the bazaar, and came back with no more definite news. She told her mistress that the parents of Kōvalaṉ and Kaṇṇaki had looked for the couple all over the city, but could find no clue as to where they might have gone.

The shocking news that Kōvalaṉ had gone back to his wife left Mātavi shattered. What would happen to her now, she worried. All she wanted was to be left alone. So she went upstairs, shut the door, lay on her bed, and cried until her eyes were red. She had no idea what to do next.

As the sun rose in the sky and the day got hotter, the news that Kaṇṇaki and Kōvalaṉ had left the city began to spread. Friends and relatives of Mātavi came to console her. She was not in any mood to see them or to be cajoled into believing that the rumour in the city was untrue, and that Kōvalaṉ would soon come back to her. Meanwhile, with Mātavi laid low, Vasantamālai was left to look after the house.

Kausikaṉ agrees to help

Chitrāpati and Mātavi had a close family friend, a young Brahmin called Kausikaṉ. When he heard that Kōvalaṉ had left Mātavi, he came to see her in the hope of bringing them together again.

When Vasantamālai announced that he had come, Mātavi brightened up and quickly came down stairs, wiping the tears from her cheeks. Kausikaṉ patiently listened to Mātavi's version of the story, which ended with Kōvalaṉ walking out in a huff.

Kausikaṉ was sure that Kōvalaṉ had acted rashly, and that Mātavi could not be blamed for the songs which she had sung by the seashore in reply to those of Kōvalaṉ. Encouraged by his reassurance, Mātavi decided to try once more to find Kōvalaṉ, and asked Kausikaṉ for his help. When he readily agreed, Mātavi was delighted and thanked him profusely. She then asked him to take a letter for her to Kōvalaṉ.

The thought that Kōvalaṉ had rejected her previous letter sent through Vasantamālai had stuck in Mātavi's mind. Although Kōvalaṉ had not read it, Mātavi did not wish to repeat its contents or its mood.

When she wrote the first time, she had not the least suspicion that Kōvalaṉ had taken the matter so seriously. Moreover, at the time when she wrote, she believed that Kōvalaṉ belonged solely to her, and that his anger was only temporary. So in that letter she had addressed Kōvalaṉ as her one true love, and used words which echoed the pleasure which they had shared.

Mātavi writes again

Now the news that Kōvalaṉ had gone back to his wife made Mātavi think again. She could no longer regard him as her rightful lover. So in her second letter she had to adopt a different approach.

"Greetings to my lord!" she wrote. "Please spare a few minutes to read these words. I do not know what drove you to hate me, but it has left me broken-hearted. I do not know either why you left the city with your wife without telling your parents. I beg you to have pity on them, and help me to understand what has happened."

In contrast to her first letter, this letter was more apologetic, suggesting that Mātavi might herself be feeling guilty. She wrote this letter on a palm leaf, and after finishing it, she read it again and again to make sure that she had not said anything that could give the slightest offence. When she was satisfied, she sealed it, and imparted to it the fragrance which she used in her hair, in the hope that the scent would remind Kōvalaṉ of their former love.

All the while, Kausikaṉ was waiting downstairs. Eventually Mātavi came down and gave him the letter enclosed in a leather envelope. She begged Kausikaṉ to try his utmost on her behalf. Promising to do no less, the young man went his way, leaving Mātavi alone with her sorrow.

Part II - Maturai

7

Kausikaṉ's errand

Unbeknown to Mātavi, Kōvalaṉ and Kaṇṇaki were already on their way to Maturai. By the time the sun was struggling to rise above the eastern horizon, they had covered about twenty miles. Kaṇṇaki was not used to walking such long distances. The soles of her feet were blistered and she felt exhausted. Leaning heavily on Kōvalaṉ's arm she asked with an innocent smile, "How much further is it to Maturai?"

Realising that she was worn out, Kōvalaṉ tried to comfort her. "It is not much further," he replied.

Kavunti Aḍikaḷ joins the travellers

As they continued their journey, they drew near to a grove of trees where there was a Jain hermitage. In that hermitage there lived a nun called Kavunti Aḍikaḷ. When they reached the place, they paid obeisance to Kavunti, who welcomed them and sat them down on a comfortable seat.

Although Kavunti was a Jain nun, she was not of a strict persuasion. At first sight, she realised that the visitors came from noble families. But from their outward appearance, she could also tell that their hearts were troubled.

"Dear children," she said, "you seem to come from good families, but you look troubled and anxious at heart. Please tell me what brought you here on foot, through jungles thick with thorns, braving highway robbers and wild beasts."

Kōvalaṉ was reluctant to open his heart at once. So he simply said that they were from Kāvirippūm Paṭṭiṉam, and that they were on their way to Maturai where he planned to set up in business. Kavunti Aḍikaḷ realised that that was not the whole story, but refrained from asking further questions. Still, she thought fit to warn them of what lay ahead.

"The distance from this hermitage to the city of Maturai is about fifty miles," she said, "but the road is rough and overgrown. The journey will be hard and dangerous, especially for Kaṇṇaki, who seems to be unaccustomed to such hardships. However, I do not expect that you will be put off by my words. But since I am planning to go to Maturai myself, perhaps I can join you. Then we can travel together until we reach that city. The journey will probably take about a week."

When Kōvalaṉ heard that Kavunti Aḍikaḷ was ready to go with them to Maturai, he felt very relieved. He hoped that Kaṇṇaki would not find the long walk so hard if she were accompanied by a wise old nun like Kavunti.

The rigours of the journey

Accordingly, on the following day Kōvalaṉ and Kaṇṇaki resumed their journey accompanied by Kavunti Aḍikaḷ. The sun was scorching hot and the road was rough. They walked in constant fear of robbers and wild animals. As far as possible, they avoided travelling during the daytime. Instead they travelled mainly at night, when it was cooler and the moon was bright.

On their way, one afternoon they came to a temple of Ko_rr_avai, the goddess of war and victory, where hunters and tribesmen of the surrounding jungle used to worship. That day was an auspicious day, and many hunters and tribal people had come to the temple with their bows and arrows.

The priestess of the temple fell into a trance, and ordered the hunters to offer animal meat to Ko_rr_avai. As she was giving these instructions, her eye fell on Kaṇṇaki. At once she returned to her rightful mind. Although she had never met Kaṇṇaki before, she spoke of her in glowing terms, describing her as a divine incarnation. Kaṇṇaki was puzzled and frightened, and clung tightly to Kōvalaṉ for protection.

After a while, the priestess and the hunters left the shrine. Kōvalaṉ then wanted to continue their journey, so as to reach Maturai as soon as possible. But Kavunti Aḍikaḷ advised him that Kaṇṇaki was too frail, and it would be better to set out again after the sun had dipped below the western horizon and the moon had risen. So after a brief rest, they took to the road again in the moonlight.

Wolves howled; owls hooted; monkeys chattered. The noises of the night made the jungle seem even more frightening. Kōvalaṉ walked beside Kaṇṇaki, holding her tightly by the arm to comfort and encourage her. For her part, Kavunti Aḍikaḷ told them edifying stories to pass the time more pleasantly, and to distract their mind from the dangers they might meet. Luckily that night they met nothing untoward.

Eventually the cocks began to crow, heralding the break of day. On hearing that, they began to walk a little faster, in order to cover as much distance as they could before the heat of the day became unbearable.

Along the road which they were following, the three travellers could find no spring or stream from which to slake their thirst. After walking for many miles, they arrived at a spot where there were a few bushes and a couple of tall trees. Complaining that she was thirsty and exhausted, Kaṇṇaki refused to go any further. Kōvalaṉ sat her down at the foot of a tree and went off in search of water, while Kavunti Aḍikaḷ stayed with Kaṇṇaki, watching the sun climb up the sky.

The long journey without proper rest or food had not only affected Kaṇṇaki, but Kōvalaṉ too. As for Kavunti, she was used to such a hard life. But Kōvalaṉ had not been able to wash or change his clothes. He looked lean and dirty, and weighed down by worry and sadness.

Kausikaṉ delivers his message

While Kōvalaṉ and his two companions were on the road to Maturai, Kausikaṉ looked for him all over Pūmpukār, carrying Mātavi's letter. When he failed to find the young couple in the city, he concluded that they must have left for Maturai. So he set out on the same road that they had taken, hoping to catch them up before long.

After journeying for many days through the jungle, Kausikaṉ saw a man in the distance, who seemed to resemble Kōvalaṉ in appearance, but he had no female companion. So when the stranger drew near, Kausikaṉ devised a test to prove to himself beyond doubt who the stranger might be. Standing by a creeper of the species known as "*mātavi*", he spoke to it aloud as though it was Mātavi herself.

"Oh *mātavi*," he lamented, "just like the dancing girl who cannot live without her lover, you too are withering, unable to bear the heat of the summer sun."

As soon as Kōvalaṉ heard mention of the word "*mātavi*", he went up to Kausikaṉ and asked him to repeat what he had said. Kausikaṉ was glad that his ruse had worked, and that he had found Kōvalaṉ alive. He then told Kōvalaṉ who he was and why he had come.

Since leaving Pūmpukār, Kōvalaṉ was not aware of what had gone on there, so Kausikaṉ told him everything. Then Kōvalaṉ realised that by leaving Pūmpukār he had caused unbearable pain to his parents, and had caused them to send messengers in all directions looking for him. Kausikaṉ described in detail Mātavi's anguish after Kōvalaṉ had deserted her. All this news made Kōvalaṉ think again about how he had treated those near and dear to him.

When Kausikaṉ saw that Kōvalaṉ was having second thoughts, he revealed that he had in fact come with a letter from Mātavi. He then slowly opened his bag and took out the leather envelope containing Mātavi's letter. Even as he took the letter from his bag, the scent it carried reminded Kōvalaṉ of the fragrance of Mātavi's hair, and brought back vivid memories of the happy years that they had spent together.

Kōvalaṉ eagerly took the letter from Kausikaṉ's hand, and broke the seal. As he read, tears fell from his eyes and he sobbed like a child. The letter made clear to him that Mātavi was blameless, and all that had happened was due to his own *karma*; it was he who was responsible for the misery that had resulted, but now it was beyond repair.

Kōvalaṉ gave no direct reply to Kausikaṉ. Instead, Kōvalaṉ told him that Mātavi's letter would explain to his parents what had happened, and asked him to deliver it to them. So Kōvalaṉ bade goodbye to Kausikaṉ and made his way back to the two women, taking some brackish water from a wayside pool in a container made from a large banyan leaf. When they had quenched their thirst, they resumed their journey.

8

Kōvalaṉ's dream

On their way, the little group met some people coming in the opposite direction. Kavunti Aḍikaḷ checked with them that they were on the right road and that Maturai was only a few miles away. The travellers assured her that they were near the city boundary, and that they had nothing more to fear. Sure enough, a few more hours' walking brought them to a grove on the outskirts of the city itself.

Kōvalaṉ and the two women were glad to rest there for a while, and to refresh themselves at a nearby spring. Although Kaṇṇaki was pleased almost to have reached their destination at last, she was totally exhausted and not in a mood to go any further.

Kōvalaṉ realised that they would now have to part company from Kavunti Aḍikaḷ, as the nun had her own matters to attend to in Maturai. So Kōvalaṉ fell at her feet and thanked her profusely for her company and for the encouragement she had given them on their long journey together.

Relieved to have reached Maturai at last in safety, Kōvalaṉ made a confession to Kavunti

Aḍikaḷ. He told her all that had happened in Pūmpukār, and how he had come to his present plight. After listening to his story, Kavunti Aḍikaḷ gave him a few words of comfort and advice.

Kavunti Aḍikaḷ blames karma

"I see that you have made serious mistakes," she said, "And you have brought on yourself great trouble as a result. This shows how strong is the influence of fate. When the consequences of one's actions in past births begin to be worked out, many people become confused due to their ignorance. They worry and suffer much as a result. The wise who are free from ignorance do not worry when this happens. To them pleasure and pain are nothing new."

Kōvalaṉ seemed less than convinced, but Kavunti Aḍikaḷ continued. "You have heard of the troubles suffered by Rama and Sita, and how king Nala lost his throne and went to the forest with his wife Damayanti? What sin did they commit to earn them such misfortune? Was it not due to fate, or to the consequences of past deeds, that both Rama and Nala were separated from their wives?

"But that is not the case with you. You are lucky! You have your wife by your side. So do not worry. Leave Kaṇṇaki here in my care, while you go to the town to find a place for you both to stay. Make sure to return before dusk falls. I will look after Kaṇṇaki until that time."

Māḍalaṉ meets the travellers

Somewhat comforted by her words, Kōvalaṉ set out to explore the city. He walked along the streets, observing the traders busily at work and wondering at the magnificent buildings on either side. After passing through the bazaar and the surrounding area of the city, Kōvalaṉ returned to Kaṇṇaki and Kavunti Aḍikaḷ and described to them all the wonders he had seen.

While Kaṇṇaki and Kavunti were listening to Kōvalaṉ's report, a Brahmin named Māḍalaṉ who had been known to Kōvalaṉ in Pūmpukār, unexpectedly came by.

In the course of conversation, Māḍalaṉ told them that he had heard all that had happened to Kōvalaṉ in Kāvirippūm Paṭṭiṉam. He sympathised with Kōvalaṉ, and said that he was saddened to hear of the troubles that had overwhelmed him. The grim situation of Kōvalaṉ and Kaṇṇaki in that grove on the outskirts of Maturai was in stark contrast to the kind of life that they had led in years gone by.

Seeing Kōvalaṉ's eyes filled with tears of remorse, Māḍalaṉ spoke to him again. "My dear Kōvalaṉ," he said, "you are no ordinary man. In the past you have supported many families, and rescued many from disaster. How can it be your destiny to suffer like this? As far as I can remember, you have always done good deeds. Why then should you suffer like this, as a beggar in an alien land? Could it really be due to your past *karma*? I cannot make it out."

Kōvalan̲'s dream forebodes ill

When Māḍalan̲ finished speaking on this note of perplexity, Kōvalan̲ told him of a dream that he had had the previous night while sleeping under a wayside tree.

"In the city of the Pāṇḍiya king," he said, "I was exposed to danger from an unscrupulous villain, and Kaṇṇaki suffered as a result. I was stripped of my clothes and forced to ride a buffalo, which is the vehicle of Yaman̲, the god of death. Kaṇṇaki and I then became ascetics, and my daughter Maṇimēkalai became a Buddhist."

Māḍalan̲ and Kavunti Aḍikaḷ were both shocked to hear Kōvalan̲'s account of his dream, Kavunti Aḍikaḷ even more than Māḍalan̲. She took the dream as portending some terrible event that was to follow. Fearing that others might get caught up in the troubles foretold by the dream, Kavunti Aḍikaḷ quickly urged Kōvalan̲ and Kaṇṇaki to leave the grove, on the grounds that it was a place for monks and nuns and holy men, and that they should seek refuge elsewhere in Maturai.

Kōvalan̲ and Kaṇṇaki had already experienced the worst that life could offer. So they did not worry about the possible dangers portended by the dream. But Kavunti Aḍikaḷ's advice left them perplexed. Even so, because she had been so good to them on their journey, Kōvalan̲ did not let her see that her words came as a surprise to him.

9

In the house of Mātari

As Kōvalan̲ and Kaṇṇaki stood there not knowing what to do next, a cowherd called Mātari passed by after delivering milk at a nearby temple. Seeing Kavunti Aḍikaḷ, she paid homage to the nun, introduced herself and stood by respectfully.

Kavunti Aḍikaḷ took a hard look at Mātari, and judged from her appearance that she was a reliable person, into whose hands Kōvalan̲ and Kaṇṇaki could safely be entrusted. So she decided to enlist her aid.

"Mātari," she said, "please listen to what I have to say. This lady Kaṇṇaki comes from a noble family. If the merchants of Maturai hear the name of Māsāttuvān̲, her father in law, they will readily welcome her and her husband, and attend to all their needs. Until they find such a home to welcome them, I entrust this lady and her husband to your care."

Kavunti Aḍikaḷ praised the qualities of Kaṇṇaki in glowing terms, so that Kōvalan̲ was astonished that she could have made so accurate an assessment of her. Mātari was spellbound. She believed every word that Kavunti Aḍikaḷ had said. As the sun was preparing to sink towards the western horizon, the cows hurried home to suckle their calves, and all around the pastures echoed with their lowing.

With a smile Mātari gestured to Kaṇṇaki and Kōvalan̲ to follow her. She beamed with joy, as if she was blessed with another daughter. On reaching her home, Mātari made a room available to Kaṇṇaki and Kōvalan̲, and provided everything to make their stay with her comfortable. Mātari already had one young daughter called Ayyai, who quickly befriended the guests. Ayyai was happy to help the newcomers and to run errands for them.

Kaṇṇaki cooks a meal

Mātari was aware that Kōvalan̲ and Kaṇṇaki would not have had a decent meal since they left Kāvirippūm Paṭṭin̲am. So she brought the necessary utensils and provisions to enable Kaṇṇaki to cook for her husband. Kaṇṇaki was delighted to be able to cook for him once again. The last time Kōvalan̲ had eaten at her hand was several years ago, on the day when Mātavi had danced before the Chōl̲a king.

Without losing a moment, Kaṇṇaki rinsed and chopped the vegetables which Mātari had supplied, and prepared various dishes that were Kōvalan̲'s favourites. Her tender hands were not used to hard work in the kitchen, as she had had many maids and servants to help her in her own household. Although her hands now became red and sore as she chopped the chillies and onions, she did not mind the pain. The thought that once again she had been blessed with the opportunity of cooking food for her husband and of serving him made up for everything.

When the rice and curry were ready, Kōvalaṉ sat down on a mat to eat, while Kaṇṇaki served the food on a plantain leaf from Mātari's garden. Kōvalaṉ ate Kaṇṇaki's food, enjoying every dish after so long an interval. Kaṇṇaki regretted that for all these years fate had prevented her from fulfilling her duty to him as his wife.

Mātari and Ayyai stood by watching as Kaṇṇaki served and Kōvalaṉ enjoyed the meal. When he had finished eating, he withdrew to another room where he sat down on a couch and talked to Ayyai.

Kōvalaṉ's confession

Soon Kaṇṇaki came in with a copper plate of betel leaves and areca nut, which she put down in front of her husband. As he chewed the betel, his mind travelled back to the past. Thinking of the way that he had acted, his eyes filled with tears. Struggling to keep control, he got up from the couch, gave Kaṇṇaki a hug and took her to one side, out of the hearing of Mātari and Ayyai.

"My parents would have been very angry that I made you walk all the way to Maturai, over a rough and stony road, among the thorns and briars," he confided. "They would have been astonished that you were able to complete so long a journey. Now I shudder to recall the hasty decision that I made back in your house in Pūmpukār.

"I do not know whether it was for good or ill. I wasted my time there and ruined my life with worthless friends. I forgot my duty, disregarded the advice of the learned, and disobeyed my parents. Above all I was unfaithful and cruel to you, my wise and noble wife.

"Little realising how badly I had acted, when finally I left Mātavi and returned to you, I told you to get ready to leave for Maturai. And without hesitation, you obeyed. I do not understand why you did so. You could easily have argued with me and challenged my decision."

Kaṇṇaki's side of the story

Kōvalaṉ's remorse moved Kaṇṇaki to the point of tears. With a catch in her voice, she replied, "Since the fatal day when you deserted me, I could no longer support Brahmins or feed the hungry. Unable to carry out those duties, I was desperately unhappy. During that time, it was your father and mother who gave me the help and support that I needed.

"I tried to hide my sorrow in their presence, and pretended that everything was all right. I put on a smile to hide my pain, but my face betrayed me. When they discovered my misery, they were deeply grieved. It was your unreasonable conduct that caused them most pain in the evening of their life.

"Although your betrayal wounded me deeply, I remained stedfast and bore it bravely. So when you said 'Come, we will go to Maturai,' I followed you dutifully."

When Kōvalaṉ heard Kaṇṇaki's words, he wept. Then with a deep sigh, he spoke to her once more.

"You have left your parents, your relatives and servants, to come with me, with nothing to protect you but your innocence and virtue," he said. "By coming with me, you have shared my burden and eased my worries. Now I cannot afford to waste any more time. I will take one of your anklets into the city, sell it there, and come back without delay. There is no need for you to worry. You can stay here happily with Mātari and Ayyai until I come back."

10

The murder of Kōvalaṉ

As Kōvalaṉ went on his way with a heavy heart, a bull stood in his path, but he did not realise that it was an omen of terrible events to come. So he came to the bazaar, and there in the street he saw a troop of men who appeared to be jewellers. They were following a leader who was so richly dressed that Kovalan guessed that he must be the royal goldsmith to the Pāṇḍiya king.

Kōvalaṉ approached him respectfully and enquired whether he was indeed the royal jeweller. "Excuse me," he said, "I have for sale an anklet that is fine enough for a queen. Could you give me an estimate of its value?" With these words, he took Kaṇṇaki's anklet from his bag and showed it to the goldsmith.

The magnificence of the golden anklet and its intricate craftsmanship took the goldsmith's breath away. He had never seen a piece like it in his life. At once his mind began to work on a cunning plan that would implicate Kōvalaṉ in the crime that he had himself just committed, and he thanked his god for showing him a way to escape from the charge that he was about to face before the king.

All the while Kōvalan̲ was wondering why the royal goldsmith remained silent, apparently lost in contemplation.

The jeweller's plot

Quickly the goldsmith came to his senses. "I was wondering who would be the most suitable person to buy an anklet of this superb quality," he said. "I have come to the conclusion that no one else could buy such a piece except a member of the royal family. My house is over there. This is my son. Please go with him, and he will make you comfortable for a short while. In the meantime I will speak to the king and queen, hear their wishes, and come back without delay."

Trusting the stranger, Kōvalan̲ followed the man's son to his house. Meanwhile the jeweller left for the palace.

He had himself stolen an anklet of the queen which had been entrusted to him for a minor repair. Until he met Kōvalan̲, he did not know what excuse he could offer to the queen for the strange disappearance of her anklet from his care. Now that Kōvalan̲ had come with this new anklet, he saw a way out of his dilemma.

The queen takes offence

When the royal jeweller entered the palace, the king was in a hall in the queen's apartments watching a programme of music and dance. The king appreciated the skill of the dancers and musicians, and lavished praise upon them.

The queen misunderstood the king's behaviour as though he was wanting to flirt with the performers, and stormed out of the hall in a rage. The king was left feeling very sorry for having given her offence, and it was while the king was in that apologetic mood that the goldsmith hurried in.

The king was irritated by his untimely intrusion, but still gave him his attention. After making obeisance to the king, the goldsmith apologised for his unannounced visit, and informed him triumphantly that he had managed to trap the burglar who had stolen the queen's anklet. He further reported that the repair which he had been employed to carry out was complete, and that he was keeping the anklet safely until it could be returned to the queen later that day.

The sentence of death

At that moment the king was preoccupied with what had just happened in the queen's apartment. So when a crime was reported which concerned the royal property, without a second thought he gave his orders: "If you find the queen's anklet in any man's possession, put him to death at once and bring me the anklet."

This was just what the goldsmith wanted to hear. Without more ado, he left the palace with a platoon of the king's guard and went straight to his house. There Kōvalaṉ was anxiously waiting for his return with good news. The sight of the guards so frightened Kōvalaṉ, that he dared not say a thing.

The goldsmith told him that the king had sent the guards to inspect the anklet in his possession, and asked Kōvalaṉ to show them the piece of jewelry. When Kōvalaṉ had duly handed it over, the goldsmith made out that a man like Kōvalaṉ could not possibly be the rightful owner of such a splendid piece of jewelry, and that the anklet must in reality belong to the queen; Kōvalaṉ therefore must have stolen it from his house while it was in his keeping for repair.

To outward appearances, Kōvalaṉ looked incapable of such a crime. So the guards refused to believe the goldsmith's accusation. The man tried to persuade them that criminals were skilled in hiding the truth, and could not be judged solely on the basis of outward appearance.

Still maintaining that Kōvalaṉ did not look like a criminal, the guards remained reluctant to carry out the sentence of death. The goldsmith insisted that Kōvalaṉ must be the thief, and if they let him go free, the king would punish them with the utmost severity.

Before the words had passed his lips, one foolhardy guardsman thrust at Kōvalaṉ with his sword, and pierced him to the heart. Kōvalaṉ fell bleeding to the ground, mortally wounded.

11

Kaṇṇaki's lament

While events were taking this tragic turn in the city, Kaṇṇaki was anxiously waiting for her husband's safe return. Although she could not tell why, she was feeling inconsolably miserable. Something told her that all was not well. Her heart was beating fast, and she was perspiring profusely.

Bad omens were occurring in the village of the cowherds where she was staying. The milk did not curdle; the eyes of the bulls ran with tears; the butter would not melt; the lambs and calves did not want to play. All these signs showed that some evil was about to befall.

Mātari, the leader of the women of the village, had met with such evil omens in the past. So she joined with the other cowgirls and prayed to Lord Kaṇṇaṉ to protect them from all ill. They performed a traditional country dance called "*kuravaik kūttu*" in which they all danced in a circle, holding hands and making a chorus of shrill sounds. When the dance was ended, Mātari went to the river Vaikai to bathe.

It was while she was bathing that Mātari heard the dreadful news: a merchant from

Kāvirippūm Paṭṭiṉam who had come to Maturai on business had been slain by the royal guards. At once she hurried back home, only to find that the women folk there were stricken with grief, for the same news had reached the village too.

All were dumbfounded. Each expected someone else to say something, but all remained silent. As Mātari's anxiety increased, she looked around fearfully to see whether Kōvalaṉ had perhaps returned. He was nowhere to be seen. She could only conclude that something had indeed gone terribly wrong.

Kaṇṇaki hears the news

In the embarrassed silence, Mātari wanted to break the news to Kaṇṇaki which she had heard at the riverside. But however much she tried, she could not utter a single word. Her whole body was trembling with shock, and she wept uncontrollably.

At last she managed to stammer out the words, "People are saying Kōvalaṉ has been killed, for stealing the anklet of the queen."

On hearing these words, Kaṇṇaki fainted. Then she rose to her feet, like a cobra that is being teased, and the tears coursed down her cheeks. She could not accept at first that her husband had been accused of theft and summarily killed without a fair trial. "Where are you, my beloved?" she cried. "What has happened to you?"

Sighing deeply, Kaṇṇaki looked around at the womenfolk who had gathered at Mātari's house to console her. Her face swollen and her eyes red with tears, Kaṇṇaki spoke to them with fury and anguish: "Mothers and sisters! You have come here to take part in the *kuravaik kūttu*, to ward off the danger that you saw coming. You performed the dance as well as you knew how. But what should never have happened, has now happened. So listen to what I have to say."

"Shall I like other women just weep and wail? Am I to bear this disgrace in silence, and let the common people regard me as the widow of a criminal? My husband met his death at the hands of the Pāṇḍiya king for no good reason. Should I not avenge his death? Should I suffer while it is the king who is the real culprit?"

Kaṇṇaki's appeal to the sun god

Then addressing the sun, she cried, "Oh sun! You are known as the god of justice. What kind of justice is this? When you know that it is the Pāṇḍiya king who is the criminal, how dare you stay silent? Will you not answer me? Should I, a stranger in Maturai, suffer like this while the king who has perverted the course of justice, continues to enjoy a life of luxury? Am I to wear the attire of a widow all my remaining days, and just wander round the country from one holy place to another? Sun, you know all that happens in this world. Now you tell me: is my husband truly a thief?"

As Kaṇṇaki finished speaking, a voice rang out from the sky: "Fair lady! Your husband is innocent.

The land that treated him as a criminal will be consumed by fire."

As soon as the sun god declared from the sky that Kōvalaṉ was innocent, Kaṇṇaki felt her burden lifted. She left the house of Mātari and began to walk the streets of Maturai, carrying in her hand her one remaining anklet, the pair to the one that Kōvalaṉ had taken to the city to sell.

As she passed along the streets, she spoke to all she met: "You chaste women of Maturai, your city is ruled by a wicked and a careless king. Listen to me carefully. This anklet which I have in my hand is the second of a pair. The other one my husband took, and tried to sell it through the treacherous goldsmith of the king."

Kaṇṇaki's vow

"I have suffered enough. There is no misery that I have not undergone. This day I have been subjected to the worst agony that any woman could ever suffer. Do I deserve it? How can it be just? Or is it due to my past *karma*?

"For whatever reason it has happened, you must understand this: my husband is no thief. A wicked man contrived a scheme to use the anklet in my husband's hand to escape from an accusation he feared would be brought against himself. He has falsely accused my husband of stealing the queen's anklet, and had him put to death. This is a gross injustice that can have no place in a country ruled by law.

"Dear women, you are chaste and virtuous. I swear before you now, that I will find my husband and hear his answer to this false charge. If I fail to do this, you can call me a liar and a lunatic."

The people of Maturai were thrown into turmoil when they heard Kaṇṇaki's bitter complaint. They believed every word she said. As well as grieving for her, they also grieved for the Pāṇḍiya king, who until that time had ruled the country with unswerving justice. In her protest, Kaṇṇaki appeared to be possessed by a divine spirit, and the people of the city feared the worst for their king and country.

Kaṇṇaki's grief beside the body of Kōvalaṉ

Out of sympathy for Kaṇṇaki, some of the women in the crowd took her to the spot where the body of Kōvalaṉ was lying.

When she saw him lying motionless in a pool of blood, she hoped that some spark of life might still be lingering in his body. She put her hand under his nose to see if he was still breathing, but there was no sign of life. Then she put her trembling hand on the left side of his chest to see if his heart was beating, however feebly. There was no sign of life there either.

Once again Kaṇṇaki was overcome with emotion. She sat down by the side of Kōvalaṉ's body, weeping and lamenting. As if he were still alive, she began to talk to him: "My dear lord!" she complained. "How could you think that I would be able to bear your loss? Does your golden body deserve to lie here in the dust? What sin have I committed to deserve this unbearable pain? Why did the king commit such a heinous crime? Cannot anyone in this city answer my questions?"

No one in the crowd dared to come forward to comfort or console her. They all stood stock still as though unaffected by her grief. Their seemingly heartless reaction to her protest threw Kaṇṇaki into a rage.

"Is there no woman here with any pity?" she cried. "Would you remain indifferent if it were your husband lying here dead? Is there no upright man in this country, who can tell right from wrong? In this city where my husband has been so brutally struck down, is there any god, any god at all?"

Kaṇṇaki sank down exhausted, and embraced the blood-soaked body of her husband. Then lo and behold! Kōvalaṉ woke from the dead and rose to his feet.

Looking directly at her, he asked her why her face had lost its glow, and wiped away her tears. Kaṇṇaki fell at his feet and grasped them tight. Looking down at her, Kōvalaṉ said, "Kaṇṇaki, my beloved, you may remain here in peace." With that, he disappeared from her sight.

Kaṇṇaki was left bemused by this experience. It seemed to her like a dream. "Could this be a miracle?" she wondered, "or has a god been deceiving me? But now more than ever, the charge against my Kōvalaṉ seems utterly unfounded. So until my rage is satisfied, I cannot go to join him. First, I must go to the king, confront him, and demand justice."

With these words, Kaṇṇaki stormed off, leaving the body of Kōvalaṉ lying in the street where he had fallen.

12

The demand for justice

As Kaṇṇaki made her way towards the palace, the Pāṇḍiya queen was in her chamber anxiously telling her maid what she had dreamt that very night.

As the maid listened attentively, the queen said, "Last night I had a most disturbing dream. His majesty's royal parasol and sceptre of justice had fallen to the ground. The bell that hangs by the palace gateway was ringing without ceasing. As I started to tremble, I saw a rainbow appear in the night sky, and a brilliant star falling from heaven in broad daylight. I fear that these are signs predicting grave danger to our king and country. I must go and tell the king what I have dreamt."

At once the queen got up and went to find her husband. When she told him her dream, the king tried to dismiss it all as pure nonsense.

At that moment Kaṇṇaki reached the palace and knocked at the gate. "Watchman!" she called. "The king whom you serve has forsaken the path of justice. Go and tell him that a widow is waiting at his gate, holding a single anklet in her hand."

Terrified by this furious woman demanding entry at the gate, the watchman hurried off to report the matter to the king. When he entered the royal presence, he could hardly put two words together.

Kaṇṇaki challenges the king

"Hail, king of Ko<u>r</u>kai!" he cried. "Hail, chief of Mount Potikai! Hail, king Neḍuñche<u>l</u>iya<u>n</u>! An infuriated woman has come to your gate. She is not Ko<u>rr</u>avai, nor is she Piḍāri, nor Kāḷi. Neither is she Durkkai, who cleft apart the chest of the demon Tāruka<u>n</u>. But she is on fire with rage, and seems intent on wreaking vengeance. In one hand she holds a golden anklet. She has demanded that I announce her arrival to your majesty."

Having heard this report, the king ordered the watchman to bring the lady in at once. Accordingly the man went out and brought Kaṇṇaki before the king, her eyes still wet with tears. Moved with sympathy for this unexpected visitor, the king asked her gently, "Young woman, why are you weeping? Who are you, and what brings you here?"

"Oh unjust king!" Kaṇṇaki replied. "Let me tell you my story. Have you heard of Sibi, who gave his life to save a dove? And of Ma<u>n</u>u Nīti Kaṇḍa Chō<u>l</u>a<u>n</u> who put his own son to death for running over a calf when driving his chariot? They were both kings of the Chō<u>l</u>a line, who ruled in Pūmpukār without a stain on their reputation.

"Kōvalaṉ, the son of Māsāttuvāṉ, was a wealthy merchant of that city. Led by fate, he came to this country of yours to earn his living. But when he tried to sell one of my anklets, he was put to death on your orders. I am his widow. My name is Kaṇṇaki."

No sooner had Kaṇṇaki finished speaking than the king gave his reply: "Punishing a criminal is no tyranny. That is plain justice, and the duty of a king."

Kaṇṇaki then played her trump card. "King of Koṟkai!" she cried. "The pair of golden anklets which I brought here with me from Pūmpukār were full of rubies."

"The queen's anklets contain pearls," the king answered, and immediately ordered his servants to bring the anklet which Kōvalaṉ had offered for sale to the goldsmith. "That anklet, the goldsmith claimed, had been stolen from the queen, and so it should have contained pearls." the king announced.

A servant brought the anklet and placed it before the king. At once Kaṇṇaki seized it and hurled it to the floor. The anklet broke apart with the impact, and the rubies it contained scattered across the floor.

The king's remorse

When the king saw the rubies, he realised that the anklet which Kōvalaṉ had offered for sale could not be the queen's, and had not been stolen from the goldsmith. Overcome by that realisation, the king cried, "How can I have acted on the word of a wretched goldsmith? It is I who am the real thief. I have failed in my duty as defender of the Pāṇḍiya realm. I cannot bear to live any longer with this shame."

With these words, he slipped down from the throne on which he had been sitting, and lay dead upon the floor. Unable to endure this sudden calamity, the queen fell down beside him and clasped his feet. Believing that no woman should survive her husband's death, there and then she too breathed her last.

13

Kaṇṇaki's revenge

After the killing of Kōvalaṉ had been avenged, Kaṇṇaki left the palace of the king, still burning with fury. The news that the king had died of shame at the injustice of his hasty order spread like wild fire. All the leading men of the kingdom gathered at the palace, while the common people came out into the streets to share the latest news. As Kaṇṇaki walked the streets of the city with dishevelled hair and tear-stained cheeks, the people came out to see her, awe-struck and bewildered. Kaṇṇaki stopped and addressed them: "Men and women of Maturai, and you gods of heaven! Listen to me. Your king has unjustly caused the death of the man I dearly loved. Therefore I curse this city, and you cannot put the blame on me for what will happen next."

Then with her own hand, she grasped her left breast and tore it from her body. Though bleeding profusely, she walked three times round the city, holding her severed breast in her hand and repeating her curse at each gate.

When she got back to her starting point, Kaṇṇaki threw away her breast, which fell in the dust of the street. At once the god of fire appeared before her, in the form of a Brahmin priest with long black curly hair. "Faithful and virtuous lady," he said, "if ever the king fails in his duty to rule justly, I have orders to burn this city to the ground. That time has now come, and I have to obey. Tell me if there is anyone whom you want me to spare."

Maturai is burnt to the ground

Kaṇṇaki was relieved that the god of fire confirmed that her cause was just. "Oh god of fire!" she replied. "Spare the Brahmins, all men of good character, virtuous women, children, cows, the disabled and the old."

Immediately the city of Maturai went up in flames, and was quickly reduced to ashes. The guardian deities of the city deserted their posts at the city gates and fled. Maturai became a ghost city, silent and empty.

Weakened by loss of blood, Kaṇṇaki walked round the burning city like a woman possessed. As she walked, the goddess of Maturai appeared before her, and told her all that had happened in her previous births, and the reasons for the troubles that had befallen her in this life. So Kaṇṇaki understood the cause of her troubles, and became calmer in her mind.

Before taking her leave, the goddess of Maturai revealed that Kaṇṇaki would meet her husband Kōvalaṉ in his heavenly form in fourteen days' time. Reassured by this, Kaṇṇaki set off in a westerly direction. After she had parted from the goddess, the fire in the city died down and burnt itself out.

Kaṇṇaki leaves the Paṇḍiya country

Near the city boundary, Kaṇṇaki saw a temple of Ko<u>rr</u>avai. Without stopping, she took off all her jewels and gold bangles and threw them into the temple compound. As she passed through the West gate of the city, she remembered the similar gate on the eastern side through which she had entered with Kōvala<u>n</u> not many days before.

"I entered this city by the East gate with my dear husband," she said to herself. "Now I am leaving it by the West gate, alone, a widow." So she walked on day and night, along the banks of the river Vaikai.

Eventually she crossed the border into the Chēra country, and reached a hill called "Tiruchenkunru". Drained of all her strength, with a great effort she climbed the hill. At the top she finally stopped, and rested beneath a *vēṅkai* tree.

It was a strange sight for the hunter people of those parts. They came running to see this beautiful young woman rapt in grief, with a bleeding wound where she had lost a breast. They came close to her, marvelling at her beauty, and asked her what had brought her there and why she seemed so sad.

Kaṇṇaki realised that they were honestly concerned for her welfare. So she answered them without bitterness. "A disaster has overtaken the city of Maturai in the Pāṇḍiya country," she said.

"It has resulted in the city being burnt to the ground. I myself am a widow, and the victim of great misfortune."

The women of the hill country were impressed by her gentle words, and moved to pity at the loss of her husband in Maturai. They saw a brightness in her face, which made them fearful, but also evoked in them the impulse to worship her.

Kaṇṇaki and Kōvalaṉ reunited

As they were gazing at her in awe, the denizens of heaven came down from the sky bringing Kōvalaṉ with them, and took Kaṇṇaki away with them in his company. The women were amazed at this sight, which convinced them that they should worship Kaṇṇaki as a goddess. In great excitement they declared that they had never seen so great a goddess in all their lives. Then they scattered through the villages of the hill country and spread the news to all the people whom they met.

The story of what the women had seen under the *vēṅkai* tree at the top of the hill Tiruchenkuṉṟu astonished all who heard it. They decided to accept the strange woman with the single breast as the special deity who would protect their villages, and all the hunter folk approved that decision without a single voice raised in opposition.

Having made this decision, the hunter folk performed their traditional dances in praise of Lord Murukaṉ and in honour of the Chēra king.

They also composed some new songs and dances in praise of the goddess with the single breast, whom they had met on the hill top.

Part III - Vañchi

14

Kaṇṇaki revered as a goddess

At that time the country adjoining the Pāṇḍiya country on its western side was the Chēra country. It was ruled by a king of the Chēra dynasty called Chēraṉ Cheṅkuṭṭuvaṉ, the son of the great Tamil emperor Imaya Varampaṉ Neḍuñchēralātaṉ.

One day Cheṅkuṭṭuvaṉ and his wife Vēṇmāḷ felt an urge to visit the hill country, to enjoy the mountain air and to see how the people of the hills were faring. So they set out from their palace in the city of Vañchi, escorted by members of the royal household. At the foot of the hills, they set up a temporary shelter and camped there for a few days.

The hunter folk of the hills heard that the king was camping nearby and came to pay him homage. The king gave his subjects the chance to air their grievances, while he listened carefully and promised them redress as soon as possible. After a friendly exchange, the king asked them whether they had any interesting news for him.

The hill people tell their story

Sensing that the king was in a favourable mood, an elderly member of the tribe bowed low before him and said, "Your majesty! We have a fascinating story to tell you. You will find it difficult to believe, but it is true.

"A couple of days ago, I and a group of our women folk climbed the hill of Tiruchenkuṉṟu to collect fire wood and to clear our plots for the sowing of hill paddy. At the top of the hill we noticed a woman standing alone under a *vēṅkai* tree. Drawn by this unusual sight, we went close to find out who she was.

"As we approached, we saw that she had lost her left breast, and all her clothes were soaked in blood. Moved by pity, we wanted to assist her. So we asked her who she was, and how she had come to be there, all alone. She was human in form, but there was an aura of divinity about her. For a while she remained silent, and gave no answer to our questions.

"Her silence filled us with awe and fear. Then, talking softly, she began to tell her story. She said that she had been widowed recently, that she had lost her husband in Maturai in the Pāṇḍiya country, and that her husband's death had resulted in the destruction of that city.

"As she finished talking, the denizens of heaven came down and gently carried her up into the sky seated in a chariot beside her husband. We do not know who she is or what country she belongs to. But never before have we seen such a strange and beautiful sight."

Cheṅkuṭṭuvaṉ praises the Pāṇḍiya king

The king was listening carefully to what the old man said. He was amazed to hear of the strange sight that the hunter folk had seen. It was almost beyond belief.

As he was trying to make sense of the story, Sāttaṉār, a learned Tamil scholar who happened to be in the king's company at that time, spoke up. He claimed to know who the lady was with but a single breast, and from what background she had come.

The king listened attentively as Sāttaṉār told the whole story of Kōvalaṉ and Kaṇṇaki from beginning to end. Particularly, the account of how the Pāṇḍiya king had met his death filled the king with awe and amazement.

Cheṅkuṭṭuvaṉ was saddened by the deaths of the Pāṇḍiya king and his wife, and by the reported destruction and misery that had befallen the people of Maturai. However, as a brother Tamil king, he felt proud of the noble example which the Pāṇḍiya king had shown.

"Neḍuñcheḻiyaṉ was truly a great king," he exclaimed. "He has done well, and I applaud his conduct. Even before the news of his fatal error had spread beyond the boundaries of his kingdom, he bade goodbye to this worldly life. By acting in this way he has restored his reputation for acting justly."

Such thoughts about the actions of the Pāṇḍiya king led the Chēra monarch to reflect on the responsibilities of kingship.

"The duties of a king are manifold," he mused. "If the rain fails, it is the king who worries most. If the people of the country suffer hardship, it is the king who feels it most keenly. It is no light task to protect the citizens of one's land from tyranny and injustice. To be born a king is indeed a heavy burden."

His queen was seated by his side, pondering the fate of Kaṇṇaki and the Pāṇḍiya queen. The king turned towards her and said, "My dear queen! You heard what Sāttaṉār said. When her husband died of shame, the Pāṇḍiya queen did not hesitate to follow him. On the other hand, Kaṇṇaki was moved by righteous indignation to avenge the death of her husband. Which of the two do you think is the greater woman?"

The queen replied without hesitation. "The Pāṇḍiya queen is no doubt a virtuous and devoted wife, worthy of respect and praise. But Kaṇṇaki is the embodiment of chastity, and a model for all Tamil women. It is these qualities that were responsible for her divine powers and her miraculous deeds. She deserves to be worshipped as a goddess."

The plan to erect a statue to Kaṇṇaki

Cheṅkuṭṭuvaṉ was pleased with the queen's reply, and looked expectantly towards his ministers. They at once understood his unspoken wish, and declared with one voice that Kaṇṇaki deserved to have a temple built for her in their country where her divinity was finally revealed.

As a first step, they proposed that a statue of the divine Kaṇṇaki should be prepared. For that purpose, a block of stone of the highest quality should be obtained, either from Mount Potikai in the South or from the Himalaya mountains in the North. If the stone were obtained from Mount Potikai, they suggested, it could be ceremonially purified by washing in the river Kāviri; if from the Himalayas, the rites could be performed in the river Ganges.

The king welcomed the suggestions of his ministers. But he dismissed the idea of obtaining the stone from Mount Potikai, since that would be below his dignity.

"Let us get the stone from the Himalayas," he concluded. "I do not think that the kings of the North will grudge us permission to take a block of the necessary size from there. If for any reason they refuse, then I may be forced to show them the mettle of the Southerners in battle, although they have had a taste of it before. I do not think that they will be so foolish as to turn down our humble request."

The king's chief minister, Villavaṉ Kōtai, then spoke for all the assembled company. He reminded the king of the victories he had won in the past, against the neighbouring Tamil kingdoms as well as against the armies of various kingdoms in the North. In those battles, the king himself had shown superhuman courage, and now there was no one who had the power to stop him if he chose to impose his rule over the whole world.

Encouraged by this support, the Chēra monarch sent letters to the rulers of the Northern kingdoms telling them of his intentions. He informed them that he would go North to the country of the Himalayas in a month's time, and he required the kings to allow him and his army free and unhindered passage. Then the king returned to his capital city with his retinue.

On the advice of his ministers, Cheṅkuṭṭuvaṉ also had a proclamation made throughout the city announcing his plan to march northward to the Himalayas. He intended that this news would be heard by the spies of the Northern kings who operated within his territory and reported to their masters.

At the same time, his court astrologer advised him that the time was auspicious and that he should now set out on his expedition without delay.

15

The expedition to the North

The news that the Chēra king was making plans to send his men to fetch a block of stone from the Himalaya mountains for a statue of Kaṇṇaki did indeed soon reach the ears of the Northern kings. The Chēra king had not declared war on them, but they had not forgotten that they had been defeated and humiliated by him only a couple of years before. So they were enraged that once again he had decided to walk into their countries as and when he pleased.

Accordingly, under the leadership of two kings, Kaṉakaṉ and Vijayaṉ, the sons of Bālakumāraṉ who had previously been defeated by Cheṅkuṭṭuvaṉ, the kings of the North met together and decided not to allow the Chēra king's men to march through their countries.

A sannyasi from the Chēra country who had been visiting Kāsi on pilgrmage at the time, happened to hear of this decision. When he returned to the South, he sought an audience with the Chēra king and told him of the decision of the Northern kings to defy him.

Cheṅkuṭṭuvaṉ's spies also, who were busy in the North gathering intelligence, sent messages confirming the report of the sannyasi.

The Chēra king was furious. He could not believe that the Northern kings could have become so bold all of a sudden. The royal priest voiced the opinion that there must have been some misunderstanding, because no one would dare to stand against a king with an unbroken record of such great victories. However, the chief astrologer declared that the time was auspicious and the king must be firm in his resolve: victory beckoned, and now was the time to march without further delay.

The march to the North

The king accepted the astrologer's advice, and decided to upset the plans of the Northern kings by making a swift attack. Losing no time, the king set out from Vañchi on his expedition with great pomp and ceremony. He ordered his sword and his royal parasol to be carried before him, and mounted on his war elephant, he set out.

As he rode away in majesty, dancers, bards and poets lined his path, proclaiming his mighty deeds on many a battlefield, while the horsemen and foot soldiers with their flashing swords shouted the praises of his prowess. The king resembled Indra, the ruler of heaven, as he set out from the celestial city to attack an army of wicked demons. The Chēra king's army was so great that it seemed to cover the whole sea-girt land. The plains shook and the mountains bowed down under its weight.

Soon with his mighty host, he reached the foot of the Nilgiri hills. There the king dismounted from his elephant, and having pitched his tent, he remained in camp there for a few days.

During that time, troupes of dancers and musicians from different parts of his kingdom came and performed before him, offering their praises and their blessings. The king rewarded each with lavish gifts of precious jewels.

Nūr̲r̲uvar Kan̲n̲ar pledges support

After the performers had left, an ambassador called Sañchayan̲, representing the Northern king Nūr̲r̲uvar Kan̲n̲ar, presented himself at Cheṅkuṭṭuvan̲'s camp. When admitted to the royal presence, Sañchayan̲ paid homage to the Chēra king and presented to him extravagant gifts as his master's tribute. He also delivered a message to the effect that Nūr̲r̲uvar Kan̲n̲ar himself was ready to obtain the required block of stone from the Himalayas, bathe it in the Ganges and personally present it to the Chēra monarch.

Cheṅkuṭṭuvan̲ thanked Nūr̲r̲uvar Kan̲n̲ar for his offer, but insisted that he had another task to perform as well as fetching the stone for the statue. That was to teach the Northern kings a lesson for their temerity.

However, the Chēra king told the ambassador that he would expect Nūr̲r̲uvar Kan̲n̲ar to make ready a fleet of barges and boats on the South bank of the Ganges, in order to transport the whole army across the river without delay as soon as it reached that point. With this message Sañchayan̲ left the camp to return to his master.

Cheṅkuṭṭuvan̲ and his army then left their camp at the foot of the Nilgiri hills and marched northwards to the banks of the Ganges. There they found the fleet of boats prepared by Nūr̲r̲uvar Kan̲n̲ar, crossed the river successfully, and continued their march.

Before they had gone very far, they were met by the army of the Northern kings. Kan̲akan̲ and Vijayan̲, the leaders of that army, were boasting, "Now we shall see how brave is this Tamil king!"

Cheṅkuṭṭuvan̲ routs his enemies

Seeing their approach, Cheṅkuṭṭuvan̲ joyfully sprang into action, like a hungry lion when it sees its prey. He ordered his forces to advance against the enemy, and the sky rang to the thunder of the drums and the clamour of the trumpets. The clouds of dust stirred up by the chariot wheels, by the elephants and horses and countless ranks of infantry, darkened the sun.

A fierce battle ensued, in which many brave soldiers on both sides lost their lives. After immeasurable slaughter both of men and animals, the army of the Chēra king gained the upper hand and the leaders of the Northern army took to flight.

Although they attempted to disguise themselves as monks and yogis, some even as musicians and dancers, fifty two of them were captured, including Kaṉakaṉ and Vijayaṉ. Finally, after seven hours of combat, the whole host of Cheṅkuṭṭuvaṉ's enemies was routed and his victory was complete.

The bathing of the stone

After gaining so decisive a victory, the Chēra king sent messengers to all those in the North country who had stood by him, to assure them of his favour. At the same time he appointed Villavaṉ Kōtai to take a detachment of soldiers to the Himalaya mountains to cut the block of stone for the statue.

When a suitable block was found and cut, it was shaped by the sculptors to the likeness of the goddess Kaṇṇaki. It was then loaded onto the heads of the defeated kings, Kaṉakaṉ and Vijayaṉ, who were compelled to carry it to Cheṅkuṭṭuvaṉ's camp on the North bank of the Ganges, as a punishment for having defied the Tamil monarch. There the statue was washed in the holy waters of the river, to purify it in accordance with the prescribed ritual.

Meanwhile, Nūṟṟuvar Kaṉṉar built a magnificent palace for the Chēra king on the South bank of the Ganges. It included spacious halls and theatres, flower gardens and lily ponds, and luxurious apartments for the king and his entourage.

Cheṅkuṭṭuvaṉ then crossed the Ganges and summoned to this newly-built palace the sons of all the soldiers who had died in the battle, and the survivors of the conflict who had performed heroically in the fight. To each one he made a generous present of gold as a reward for their services, while the court bards sang his praises.

16

A report from Pūmpukār

After the ceremony was over, with the Chēra king seated on his throne, the Brahmin Māḍalan̲ came into his presence. "Long live the king!" he said. "The song sung on the seashore has caused a heavy burden to fall on the heads of Kan̲akan̲ and Vijayan̲."

"You speak in riddles," replied the king. "Explain what you mean." Although he was aware of what had happened in Maturai, the king did not know of all that had gone before, to bring Kōvalan̲ and Kaṇṇaki to that city.

In obedience to the king's command, Māḍalan̲ told him what had happened in Pūmpukār, of Kōvalan̲'s marriage to Kaṇṇaki, how he had deserted her to live with Mātavi and then returned to her after the incident on the seashore. He then went on to explain what had brought him to see the king at the present time.

The aftermath of Kōvalan̲'s death

Māḍalan̲ recounted how, when passing through Maturai, he had heard the fate of the cowherd, Mātari. On hearing what had happened to Kōvalaṉ and Kaṇṇaki in that city, Mātari had apparently felt such intense remorse for having failed to protect the girl entrusted to her care that she took her own life by throwing herself into the fire. Moreover, Kavunti Aḍikaḷ, the Jain nun who had accompanied the couple on their journey to Maturai, unable to bear her sorrow at the tragic events, had fasted unto death.

That was not all he had to tell. When he heard what had happened to his son, Māsāttuvāṉ, Kōvalaṉ's father, was overcome with despair. He gave away all his earthly goods and entered a monastery to live as an ascetic. His wife died of sorrow. Māṉāykaṉ too, Kaṇṇaki's father, had taken up the life of an ascetic, and her mother also had died shortly afterwards.

When this news reached the ears of Mātavi, according to Māḍalaṉ's account, she went to her mother Chitrāpati and begged her not to allow her daughter Maṇimēkalai to enter the life of a courtesan, which could only lead to unhappiness. She herself then shaved off her hair and entered a Buddhist nunnery.

Since it was he himself who had brought news of the terrible events in Maturai to Pūmpukār, and had thereby caused this further cycle of misfortunes, Māḍalaṉ told the Chēra king that he was now travelling northwards to the Ganges, to bathe in its waters and thereby to purify himself of the guilt that he had incurred.

Having shared all this shocking news, Māḍalaṉ was about to take leave of the king and depart. Before he could do so, Cheṅkuṭṭuvaṉ stopped him and asked a further question: "Can you tell me what happened in the Pāṇḍiya country after its king had met his death?"

"After the destruction of the city by fire," replied the Brahmin, "Ve<u>rr</u>ivē<u>r</u> Che<u>l</u>iya<u>n</u> came to the throne and sacrificed a thousand goldsmiths in a single day. It is hoped that the new king will restore the Pāṇḍiya kingdom to its former glory."

Cheṅkuṭṭuva<u>n</u> sets out for home

At this point, the court astrologer stood up and reminded the Chēra king that he had been absent from Vañchi for thirty-two months. So the king gave Māḍala<u>n</u> a present of gold equal to his own weight, and sent him on his way.

Cheṅkuṭṭuva<u>n</u> allowed Nu<u>rr</u>uvar Ka<u>nn</u>ar and the other allied kings from the North who had gathered at his camp to return to their own countries. He sent ahead the captured kings, however, including Ka<u>n</u>aka<u>n</u> and Vijaya<u>n</u>, to the capitals of the Pāṇḍiya and Chō<u>l</u>a kings as trophies of war, in the custody of his general, Nīla<u>n</u>. The following morning as the sun rose, leading his victorious army, Cheṅkuṭṭuva<u>n</u> set out for the South.

17

A temple for Kaṇṇaki

There were great celebrations in the Chēra capital when Cheṅkuṭṭuvan̲ and his soldiers reached the city of Vañchi. He was warmly welcomed by his queen, Vēṇmāḷ, who had been pining for the day of his return, and by troupes of dancers and musicians. The celebrations lasted for many days.

In the midst of the festivities, the king was informed of the return to his palace of Māḍalan̲ and of Nīlan̲, who had escorted Kan̲akan̲ and Vijayan̲ to the courts of the other two Tamil kings.

Nīlan̲ brought the sombre report that both the Chōl̲a and the Pāṇḍiya kings had spoken disparagingly of the action of Cheṅkuṭṭuvan̲ in sending to them the captured kings in chains. They could not see the merit of having taken prisoner these enemy kings who had shown so little courage on the battlefield.

At first, on hearing this, the Chēra king was enraged and his eyes flashed fire. However, Māḍalan̲ came forward to assuage his wrath. He reminded him of all the victories and the fame that he had won, and advised him not to take the jealous response of the other Tamil kings too seriously.

Accepting the wisdom of the Brahmin's words, Cheṅkuṭṭuvaṉ soon cooled down. Realising the futility of war and bloodshed, he ordered the release of all the captured Northern kings from prison, and promised that they would be sent back to their own lands.

The consecration of Kaṇṇaki's temple

Then without more ado, Cheṅkuṭṭuvaṉ instructed his ministers to build a temple to Kaṇṇaki, in which her new image was to be installed. Accordingly, under the guidance of the priests and astrologers, a magnificent temple was built in her honour, in accordance with the prescribed rules. When the work was completed, on an auspicious day and time, the temple was consecrated in the presence of the Chēra monarch.

With the consecration of the new temple successfully completed, Cheṅkuṭṭuvaṉ was satisfied that he had proved his religious devotion as well as his prowess in war. The news that he had built a temple to Kaṇṇaki in his capital spread throughout the length and breadth of India. Soon kings and lords from many nations round about were coming to Vañchi to offer their prayers to the goddess.

Encouraged by its popularity, the Chēra king conceived the desire to establish in the new temple a regular daily round of prayer and worship. In order to involve as many people as possible in this undertaking, and to ensure their support, he called a meeting of kings and priests and astrologers to draw up a plan.

The arrival of Tēvanti

While all this was going on, Tēvanti, the companion of Kaṇṇaki, together with her foster mother and another of her close friends, came to hear how Kōvalaṉ had met his death and how the city of Maturai had been burnt to the ground. So they set out from Pūmpukār to look for Kaṇṇaki. On reaching Maturai, they heard of the death of the herdswoman Mātari, and visited her daughter Ayyai.

Ayyai told Tēvanti and her companions that Kaṇṇaki had left for the hill country to the West. So the three of them accompanied by Ayyai travelled westward from Maturai along the banks of the river Vaikai until they came to the hill of Tiruchenkuṉṟu. The people of that place told them that Kaṇṇaki was now revered as a goddess, and that the Chēra king had built a splendid temple in her honour.

Emboldened by this news, the four women hurried on to Vañchi where they made their way to the royal palace and there were granted access to the presence of the king. Each of them in turn introduced themselves to the monarch, explaining their connection to the goddess and expressing their grief for all that had happened.

At this point, it seemed fitting for the king with his courtiers and the four visitors to proceed together to the temple of the goddess, and there they prostrated themselves before her image in adoration. As they did so, Kaṇṇaki herself appeared before them in the heavens in her celestial form.

The goddess speaks from heaven

Cheṅkuṭṭuvaṉ was overwhelmed by the beauty of the vision, and cried out in wonder and amazement. The voice of the goddess was then heard from heaven, speaking to reassure her devotees: "Neḍuñcheḻiyaṉ, the former Pāṇḍiya king, is free from any blame, and he now lives with Indra in heaven as his guest. I myself am regarded as his daughter, and I shall for ever play upon the hill of the Lord Murukaṉ. Come, my friends, and join me there!"

When they heard the goddess speak, Tēvanti and her companions were spell-bound, and sang an ecstatic hymn of praise in her honour. Then, in answer to the king's enquiry about Maṇimēkalai, Tēvanti told him what had happened to Mātavi and her daughter.

As she finished her story, she fell into a trance and was possessed by the spirit of the god, Pāsaṇṭa Sāttaṉ. While under the influence of the god, Tēvanti revealed many strange and wonderful things, to the amazement of Cheṅkuṭṭuvaṉ and all who heard her.

The Chēra king was now doubly convinced that Kaṇṇaki was a goddess worthy of veneration.

So with the agreement of all those who had come to consult with him, he decreed that daily worship be offered to the goddess under the name of Pattiṉi Tēvi, the goddess of faithfulness. He also appointed Tēvanti to be responsible for the offering of flowers, incense and perfume in her shrine.

Then Cheṅkuṭṭuvaṉ walked three times round the sanctuary and bowed before the image of the goddess. The Northern kings, now released from prison, and those who had come to plan with him for the regular offering of worship in the temple, including Gajabāhu, king of Sri Lanka, joined him in adoration.

As they did so, they made the fervent prayer that the goddess would manifest her presence in their countries as she had done in the Chēra land. In response, a gracious voice was heard from heaven saying, "All your requests are granted."

THE DANCING GIRL'S DAUGHTER

1

Mātavi and the music festival

Chōḻa Nāḍu, the country of the Chōḻa kings, was famous for its fertility and for the learning of its people. The capital of the Chōḻa country was Pūmpukār, which in former times was known as Sampāpati, after the goddess of that name who was its guardian. It was in this city that the series of memorable events already told had begun, though the final event of that story happened in the country of the Chēra kings.

The main characters of that earlier story, Kōvalaṉ, Kaṇṇaki and Mātavi, were all born and bred in Pūmpukār. Kōvalaṉ, the husband of

Kaṇṇaki, deserted his wife and lived with the courtesan called Mātavi.

The women of the courtesan caste were the custodians of Tamil fine arts, such as music and dance. It was through their devotion to those art forms that Tamil music (now called Carnatic music) and Tamil dance (called Bharatha Natyam) have come down to us.

The love between Mātavi and Kōvalaṉ resulted in the birth of a baby girl, whom Kōvalaṉ named Maṇimēkalai after his own tutelary deity. The child was blessed with matchless beauty and a pleasant character, and she blossomed into an accomplished girl with a special interest in philosophy. However, since she was born into a family of courtesans, her grandmother Chitrāpati took every step to ensure that she became a skilled dancer and entertainer like her mother Mātavi. Accordingly, from an early age Maṇimēkalai learned music and dance from great classical teachers, and grew up to be a credit to her family.

It was just at the point when Maṇimēkalai was being groomed to become an outstanding performer that her father Kōvalaṉ deserted her mother Mātavi and returned to Kaṇṇaki, his lawful wife. Together Kōvalaṉ and Kaṇṇaki then went off to the city of Maturai in the Pāṇḍiya country, and there Kōvalaṉ was charged with the offence of stealing the jewelry of the queen and put to death.

When Mātavi heard of the death of Kōvalaṉ, she felt deeply sorry, and all desire for her former way of life evaporated. In her misery she consulted a Buddhist monk called A<u>r</u>avaṇa Aḍikaḷ, whose words of wisdom brought comfort to her grieving heart. The philosophy of the Buddha appealed to her, and she began to wonder whether his teaching might give permanent solace to her troubled mind.

Mātavi's hatred for the courtesan life was such that she seriously questioned whether her daughter Maṇimēkalai should be allowed to follow the traditional path. After several weeks of reflection, Mātavi made up her mind and shaved her head. After listening to her mother and seeing her dispirited state of mind, Maṇimēkalai's too began to waver.

While Mātavi was being tossed about by questions such as these, the season for the festival of Indra arrived, which was to last for twenty-eight days. From the time that Mātavi became the mistress of Kōvala<u>n</u>, she had regularly been taking part in the festival, giving dance performances and musical recitals at various venues around the city. News of Kōvala<u>n</u>'s death and the destruction of the city of Maturai had shaken her to the core, and now she was left without any hope or purpose.

Mātavi's renunciation

In the past Mātavi would have had several engagements to perform in public during the season of the Indra festival. This year however, as she was still wrapt in her thoughts about Kōvala<u>n</u>, the music and dance companies did not invite her to perform at all.

The public was quite unaware of her mood, and was expecting that like any other courtesan she would sing and dance as she had done in the past. However, when people realized that Mātavi was not going to perform at any of their concerts, they were very disappointed. Her absence from the dance halls revived the talk about her life with Kōvalaṉ, and about all the other events involving Kōvalaṉ and Kaṇṇaki.

Chitrāpati, the mother of Mātavi, was more worried than any one else. She did not dare to talk to Mātavi about it for fear of being rebuffed. In her heart of hearts, Chitrāpati was concerned that Maṇimēkalai too might follow Mātavi's example and bring discredit to her caste. So she decided on a subterfuge, and summoned Vasantamālai, a companion of Mātavi, whom she knew was the one person to whom Mātavi would give ear, even if she did not heed what she was told.

When Vasantamālai came, Chitrāpati tried to persuade her that what Mātavi was doing was wrong and unfair to the art lovers of Pūmpukār. Partly convinced by Chitrāpati's arguments, Vasantamālai went to meet Mātavi.

When she learnt that Mātavi was not at home, Vasantamālai made enquiries and was told that she had gone to the Buddhist nunnery with Maṇimēkalai. After searching the whole place, Vasantamālai came at last to a shed in the garden where Mātavi and Maṇimēkalai were busy weaving garlands of flowers.

At once Mātavi welcomed Vasantamālai, and when she had sat her down, they exchanged the usual pleasantries. Vasantamālai was pained to see how thin Mātavi had become. Her thoughts flashed back to the years when Mātavi was the very embodiment of good cheer, always bubbling with laughter and jokes.

Vasantamālai remained silent and looked away, until Maṇimēkalai broke the silence with the question, "What news is there from the town?"

The opportunity which Vasantamālai was waiting for came, and she slowly began to speak: "The Indra festival is in progress. Although it has reached its tenth day it has not yet become lively or entertaining. The dance performances around the city are quite dull and unattractive. Lovers of music and dance came in search of their accustomed pleasures, but they have been frustrated.

"Moreover, rumours abound that Mātavi may not perform at this year's festival at all, and that is extremely irritating for the connoisseurs of the arts. The public appears to be of the view that it is not right for you to forsake the traditional duty of performing, even though you may have your own personal reasons for doing so.

"Please bear with me, Mātavi, if I tell you that I share the public's view. You must know that your mother too is really disturbed by your indifference to public opinion in this matter. By remaining aloof and shutting yourself away like this, you will only heighten your own grief and pain. Time alone can ease your sadness and bring solace to your heart.

As you know, I only mean well for you. Please cheer up, and shake off this reclusive mood."

After listening patiently to all Vasantamālai's arguments, Mātavi began talking sadly about the greatness of Kaṇṇaki, and how by dint of her chastity and virtue she had destroyed the city of Maturai. In that way she had proved the innocence of her husband Kōvalaṉ to the entire world.

Mātavi confided to Vasantamālai that after listening to Aṟavaṇa Aḍikaḷ she had now converted to Buddhism, and that it was her intention to lead Maṇimēkalai also on the same path of enlightenment. She declared her belief that the life of a courtesan was despicable, and announced her firm decision to forsake it for ever.

Finally Mātavi said, "Vasantamālai! You have been such a good friend to me all these years. I am really sorry that I cannot please you this once. Please go and tell my mother and all my relatives and friends that Mātavi and Maṇimēkalai are firm in their decision, and that they will not swerve from the path on which they have now set out. God be with you! Please leave us now."

Vasantamālai bowed to Mātavi and took her leave, deeply frustrated and with a heavy heart.

2

In the Uvavaṉam gardens

Until Mātavi mentioned the terrible events in Maturai involving Kaṇṇaki and her father Kōvalaṉ, Maṇimēkalai had no inkling of them. When she heard her mother talk about it to Vasantamālai, she was horrified. Her face was wet with tears, and a few pearly drops rolled down onto the garland of flowers which she was weaving.

Noticing this, Mātavi felt that the garland had been polluted, and so had become unsuitable for offering in worship. She wiped away Maṇimēkalai's tears and comforted her. Then, since they had not picked enough flowers for another garland, Mātavi asked her daughter to go back to the garden to pick some more.

When Maṇimēkalai's companion Sutamati overheard what Mātavi was saying, she broke in and warned against sending Maṇimēkalai alone to the garden. She said that recently the garden had become the haunt of rowdy youngsters, so it would not be safe for a young girl like Maṇimēkalai to visit the place on her own without an escort. Sutamati said that she had ample reason for this advice, and backed it up with her own personal experience:

"I come from the city of Saṇpai," she said, "and I am the daughter of a Brahmin called Kausikaṉ. One day while I was picking flowers in the garden, a celestial being called Mārutavēkaṉ came down from the sky on his way to Pūmpukār to enjoy the festival of Indra.

"As soon as he saw me all alone in the garden, he landed on the ground by my side, seized me forcibly and before I could raise a cry for help, he carried me off to his celestial abode. There, much against my wish, he kept me by force and had his way with me. Having kept me there for a few weeks, he brought me back and left me at the same spot where he had first set eyes on me."

The visit to Uvavaṉam

Sutamati's sad story made Mātavi take her warning seriously. She thanked Sutamati for her timely suggestion and asked her to go with Maṇimēkalai and to look after her wherever she went. Accordingly Maṇimēkalai set off for the garden escorted by her companion.

Now Sutamati was very familiar with all the parks and gardens in the area, and she showed Maṇimēkalai around, telling her which ones were forbidden and which flowers grew where.

Eventually after a long walk, the two girls saw a garden in the distance called Uvavaṉam. Sutamati assured Maṇimēkalai that Uvavaṉam was the only garden which was not frequented by rowdy people, owing to the strictness of the wardens of the place, and that every variety of fragrant flower could be found there. Sutamati went on to say that Uvavaṉam was famous for other reasons also:

"In that garden, there is a hall built entirely of crystal, the Crystal Hall (*paliṅkaṟai maṇḍabam*)," she told Maṇimēkalai.

"Within that hall there is a shrine called the Lotus Altar (*tāmarai pīḍikai*)," she continued. "There worshippers come to venerate the feet of the Lord Buddha. If flower buds are placed on it they will bloom at once, and will never wither as long as they remain there; nor will those flowers attract bees or beetles. It is believed that the altar has been blessed by the Lord Buddha himself, and has magic powers."

The popular gossip

As the two of them were heading towards the entrance to Uvavaṉam, they saw all manner of people whiling away their time looking at the pictures painted on the walls of the houses along the path. Some of them appeared to know Maṇimēkalai as the only daughter of the famous dancer called Mātavi.

On seeing Maṇimēkalai, they began to talk about her mother's decision to become a Buddhist, and about her attempt to persuade Maṇimēkalai to do the same. They branded Mātavi as cruel, and said that she had no right to force her daughter to follow in her own footsteps.

As the girls passed by, the common people commented on Maṇimēkalai's exceptional beauty, and repeated that she should have the right to enjoy worldly pleasures according to her own wishes. Sutamati and Maṇimēkalai could hear all these remarks, but went on their way without taking them to heart, because they could see that they were made without any malice.

Eventually they entered the garden, and found it thick with tall trees, bushy shrubs and twining creepers. It seemed as if the darkness itself had taken refuge there, fearing the fierce rays of the sun.

Birds and insects found sanctuary in the garden, and felt at home in its shade. Dragon flies, beetles and bees were buzzing around singing tunefully, each in its own musical mode. Under the canopy of the trees, which gave the impression of a cloudy sky, peacocks danced and the monkeys in the tree tops admired the beauty of their dance.

Sutamati and Maṇimēkalai walked through the garden enjoying these pleasant scenes without a care.

3

Utayakumaraṉ's first approach

Many were the men who longed to have Maṇimēkalai as their lover, and foremost among them was Utayakumaraṉ, the son of the Chōḻa king. In that land, Utayakumaraṉ was known for his prowess and valour, and for his skill in riding elephants.

The chief elephant of the king was called Kāḷavēkam. On the day when the two girls visited Uvavaṉam to gather flowers, Kāḷavēkam was in must, and in a dangerous frenzy was harrassing everyone in the street. While its accustomed mahouts tried vainly to subdue the beast, it ran amok knocking over everything that stood in its way.

The news that the elephant was wreaking such havoc reached the ears of prince Utayakumaraṉ. At once he rushed out into the street only to see the elephant speeding on, trampling everything in its path. Utayakumaraṉ gave chase with fiersome cries, but Kāḷavēkam only sped on at an ever faster pace. Finally the elephant became tired, and calmed down a little.

Snatching the opportunity, Utayakumaraṉ mounted the elephant and with the help of the goad directed the elephant to its stall and tethered it there. The people of the town and the mahouts who had run for their lives, breathed a sigh of relief and heartily congratulated the prince on his achievement.

Mightily pleased with himself, Utayakumaraṉ was returning to the palace when in a certain street in the city notorious for its courtesans, he saw through the window of a house the face of his friend, Eṭṭikumaraṉ. Their eyes met, and at once Eṭṭikumaraṉ came out and greeted the prince. As they were men of like mind who were for ever indulging in sensual pleasures, Eṭṭikumaraṉ broke the news that he had seen Maṇimēkalai and Sutamati entering Uvavaṉam.

The mention of Maṇimēkalai stoked the flames of desire that were already smouldering in the prince's heart. He imagined that the garden would be an ideal place for him to persuade Maṇimēkalai to yield to his wishes. Unable to contain his desire, Utayakumaraṉ gallopped off towards Uvavaṉam on his horse.

Utayakumaraṉ tries to meet Maṇimēkalai

It was unusual for anyone to enter Uvavaṉam on horseback, so the sound of the horse's hoofs at once drew the attention of Sutamati and Maṇimēkalai.

The latter had already heard that the prince had been trying to woo her. She was also aware that he had spoken to her grandmother Chitrāpati with a view to asking for her hand, and that her grandmother had promised to persuade the girl to become the prince's partner.

Therefore, fearing that the sound she heard could be that of the prince's horse approaching, Maṇimēkalai anxiously asked Sutamati for help to find a way out of the imminent danger.

Sutamati herself began to tremble like a peacock chased by dogs, and racked her brains to find a way of escape. Suddenly there came to her mind the thought of the Crystal Hall which stood in Uvavaṉam and enclosed the Lotus Altar, and she quickly advised Maṇimēkalai to take refuge there.

After making sure that Maṇimēkalai had entered that place of safety, she moved away and pretended to be gathering flowers nearby. All the while she kept a wary eye on developments.

The prince looked everywhere for Maṇimēkalai, and soon spotted Sutamati by a jasmine creeper. He recognized her at once, dismounted from his horse, and approached her. He hoped that he could gain his end by speaking to Sutamati whom he knew to be a bosom friend of Maṇimēkalai.

The prince's approach made Sutamati's heart beat rapidly in fear. He foolishly imagined that she had brought Maṇimēkalai to the garden with the specific purpose in mind of introducing her friend to him. He knew that as a man he was debarred from entering the precincts of the Buddhist nunnery where Mātavi and Maṇimēkalai were staying. He further assumed that Sutamati must deliberately have chosen Uvavaṉam as the best place for such an introduction. So he addressed her brightly:

"My dear Sutamati! When I saw you alone in this garden, I could guess what you and your companion Maṇimēkalai had in mind. Maṇimēkalai's grandmother will have told you of my love for her grand-daughter. I believe that it was to make known her love to me in person that Maṇimēkalai has come here with you now. Have I not read the situation aright?"

Sutamati foils the prince

The prince spoke in a tone of innocent expectation, but the hollowness of his words shocked Sutamati. She wondered why the prince should build such castles in the air, and determined then and there to prick the bubble of his hopes. In an attempt to put him off from his impossible quest without more ado, she made her reply.

"May it please you, your excellency," she said, "You come from an illustrious line, and your family enjoys a glorious reputation. Because your ancestor Karikālaṉ believed that the rule of law should prevail, and that justice should not only be done but should also be seen to be done, he disguised himself as an old man and dispensed justice without fear or favour.

"You are a worthy descendant of Karikālaṉ. As one who has herself been defiled by a celestial being, it is not fitting for me to offer advice to a prince like yourself. However, our human bodies are no more than superficial decoration. When they fade, we are only a mass of flesh and bones riddled with waste products. What value does this body have in old age? What use is there in seeking to prolong our youth and beauty?"

Sutamati went on talking in this vein, but the prince was in no mood to listen to her exhortations. His eyes were searching for Maṇimēkalai. Suddenly he saw her inside the Crystal Hall. Forgetting that Sutamati was talking to him, the prince was beguiled by Maṇimēkalai's beauty, and longed to make her his own by hook or by crook.

Although Sutamati confirmed that Maṇimēkalai had decided to follow her mother's path and become a nun, Utayakumaraṉ imagined that he could win her if only Sutamati would cooperate with him. So he began to coax Sutamati into a conversation, and asked for personal details about herself.

For a start, acknowledging that Sutamati herself had a reputation for celestial beauty, he asked her why she should want to associate with someone like Mātavi who had converted to Buddhism.

Sutamati reveals her past

Since Utayakumaraṉ spoke in a way that gave the impression of genuine sympathy and concern, Sutamati was emboldened to tell him her story:

"I lost my mother when I was very young," she began. "She was a strong lady, who guided the household with a firm hand. Her death devastated my father, and he lost his grip on life. Eking out a meagre existence by performing religious sacrifices and rituals as a priest, he forgot about his daughter and left me to fend for myself. He would go to distant places and spend months away, leaving me in the care of distant relatives. So I grew up on my own, and lost touch with him completely.

"After living in the North of India for a couple of years, he came back to the South with pilgrims on their way to Kaṉṉiyākumari. While he was passing through the place where he was born, he learnt that I was still alive and living in that very city. When he heard that I had been defiled by a celestial being, he wept tears of sorrow for his past irresponsibility and for neglecting his duty as a father.

"Since I was regarded as impure, I was thought unfit to lead a normal family life, and it was this that compelled me to join a Jain nunnery. While I remained there, my father lived in a separate house nearby, depending on others for his living. It gave him great pleasure to meet me every day in the monastery.

"One day, a mad cow chased my father, butted him and tore his stomach open. As there was no one to give immediate help, he came to the monastery close to where I was staying, holding his entrails in his hand. The monks and nuns in the monastery refused to give him any assistance. When I pleaded with them to show mercy, they drove me out of the premises along with my father, who was fighting for his life.

"As we left the monastery, we were walking along the street looking for some kind soul to come to our aid. At a distance we saw a Buddhist holy man in yellow robes coming towards us with a begging bowl in his hand. When he came up with us, he saw my father's plight. Losing no time, he passed me his begging bowl, lifted my father onto his shoulders and hurried to a nearby Buddhist temple. There the monks gave my father the assistance he needed, and by their prompt action saved his life.

"In an effort to repay the monks of the Buddhist temple for the timely help they had given, I decided to remain there and to offer whatever service I could. It was while I was there that I got to know Mātavi and Maṇimēkalai. I too have now embraced Buddhism, and have found solace and peace of mind through that religion."

Utayakumaraṉ gives up

Sutamati's words did not please Utayakumaraṉ. He felt that she was not minded to help him achieve his aim. So he left the garden disappointed, thinking that Chitrāpati alone would now be able to help him.

When she saw Utayakumaraṉ depart, Maṇimēkalai came out of the Crystal Hall where she had taken refuge. She was pulled this way and that by conflicting feelings. Although she was on the verge of becoming a Buddhist nun, she was not truly free from worldly desires. Inexplicably, she felt strongly attracted by Utayakumaraṉ.

So she confided to Sutamati, "Although Utayakumaraṉ despises me as unchaste and irreligious, and criticizes me for being a social rebel, strangely enough, my heart is still set on him. Perhaps that is a sign that earthly love still has a hold on me. If that is so, may I be soon set free from its demeaning bondage!"

Maṇimēkalā Teyvam appears

When she had finished speaking, Maṇimēkalai paced up and down wondering why her mind was still tossed to and fro. At that moment, the goddess Maṇimēkalā Teyvam, who had come down to earth to enjoy the Indra festival, entered the Crystal Hall from which Maṇimēkalai had just emerged.

The goddess walked reverently around the Lotus Altar and then left the Hall. When the sun started to sink into the Western ocean, Maṇimēkalā Teyvam assumed the form of a beautiful woman and hastened to the place where Sutamati was standing by herself.

Addressing Sutamati politely, she asked who she was and why she was standing there alone at that time. She went on to ask whether she was lost and needed help. The strange woman's words were so kind and caring that Sutamati was emboldened to tell her without any reservation who she was, how she came to be in the garden, and why she was looking so anxious. The disguised goddess listened patiently, while

Maṇimēkalai watched the converstation from a little way off.

"From what you tell me," said Maṇimēkalā Teyvam, "it is very clear that Utayakumaraṉ has fallen passionately in love with Maṇimēkalai, and since he is a prince, he must be capable of carrying out whatever he wants. It is only because of his respect for the ascetics in this place that he has left without resorting to force.

"Tonight the moon will be full, so it is probable that he will lie in ambush outside the garden with his retinue of guards. I cannot say anything for sure, but to be forewarned is to be forearmed. You should not return home by the same route as the one by which you came.

"On the Western side of this garden there is a small gate. If you pass through that gate, it will take you straight to the area called the Chakkaravāḷa Kōṭṭam. From there you can go on your way without fear."

Maṇimēkalā Teyvam plays a trick

Sutamati was grateful for the kind advice given her by the goddess in disguise. However, she was puzzled to hear the words "Chakkaravāḷa Kōṭṭam" from the mouth of this strange woman. So she politely asked the stranger why she referred to that place as Chakkaravāḷa Kōṭṭam (which means abode of the celestials) when everyone else called it Suḍukāṭṭuk Kōṭṭam (cremation ground).

The strange lady began to explain why Chakkaravāḷa Kōṭṭam was also known as Suḍukāṭṭuk Kōṭṭam, and went on to describe its history in detail. All this was so tedious that Sutamati dozed off to sleep. Snatching this opportunity Maṇimēkalā Teyvam made Maṇimēkalai fall into a trance and carried her away to a nearby island called Maṇipallavam, where she set her down in a place of safety.

Still under the goddess's spell Maṇimēkalai slept there peacefully. Allowing her to sleep on without disturbing her, Maṇimēkalā Teyvam returned to Pūmpukār to give advice to Utayakumaraṉ.

The goddess woke him up while he was having sweet dreams about Maṇimēkalai. She advised him that it was futile for him to desire a girl who had given herself over to the cause of Buddhism, and so he should stop pursuing her any further. The goddess's advice was like blowing a conch into the ears of the deaf.

4

Sutamati receives divine instruction

After advising Utayakumaraṉ to follow the path of virtue, still in her disguise Maṇimēkalā Teyvam returned to the place where Sutamati was sleeping and gently woke her up. Sutamati was startled to see the same strange lady standing by her side.

The goddess now assumed her real form once more, and said that she had come to see the Indra festival at Pūmpukār, and moreover she was fully aware of all the trials and tribulations that Maṇimēkalai had undergone. She added that there was every chance of Maṇimēkalai being accepted as a Buddhist nun, and that it was she who had carried her away from the Lotus Altar to a place of safety. As Sutamati listened in wonder, Maṇimēkalā Teyvam continued:

"I have taken Maṇimēkalai to the island of Maṇipallavam for a particular purpose," she said. "There she will learn about her previous birth, and in seven days' time she will return to Pūmpukār. On the day of her return, you will witness many supernatural events. If you meet Mātavi, tell her that it was I who took Maṇimēkalai to Maṇipallavam.

"Mātavi is no stranger to me. After the birth of their daughter, Kōvalaṉ and Mātavi were racking their brains to choose a suitable name for the baby girl. Then it was Kōvalaṉ who suggested that she should be given my name, since I was his tutelary deity.

"On the day that Maṇimēkalai was named, I appeared to Mātavi in a dream and congratulated her for bringing forth so fine a child as Maṇimēkalai. Please remind Mātavi of all these things so that she will remember who I am."

With these words, Maṇimēkalā Teyvam took her leave, but for Sutamati it all seemed like a dream.

Sutamati reaches Chakkaravāḷa Kōṭṭam

As Maṇimēkalā Teyvam had advised, Sutamati left the Crystal Hall and passed through the small gate out of the Uvavaṉam gardens. When she reached the Chakkaravāḷa Kōṭṭam, she sat down quietly by the side of the house called Ulaka Aṟavi. This was a place of refuge where the sick and needy came to find shelter and support.

Close to this house there was a temple dedicated to the goddess Sampāpati, which had many pillars. Attached to one of the pillars was a statuette fashioned by Māyaṉ, the celestial architect. This statuette had the power of speech, and like an oracle could foretell the future, as well as revealing the details about people's past lives. All of a sudden, to Sutamati's amazement, the statuette began to speak.

"Dear daughter of King Ravivaṉmaṉ, and wife of Tuchayaṉ!" it began. "How are you? I am now going to tell you something that will be quite new to you.

"In your previous birth your name was Vīrai. You had an elder sister called Tārai, who was killed by an elelphant. Unable to bear your grief at her loss, in due course you also died. In this birth you have been born as the daughter of Kausikaṉ, with the name of Sutamati, while your sister Tārai has now been born as Mātavi.

"In your previous birth, you had another sister too, whose name was Lakshmi. She has now been born as the daughter of Mātavi, and her name is Maṇimēkalai. She is now on an island four hundred miles away, but in seven days' time, she will arrive here. She too will have been told by me about her previous birth. You have nothing to fear; so be of good heart!"

After revealing the past and foretelling the future, the statuette went silent, leaving Sutamati bewildered. She eagerly waited for the night to pass and the new day to dawn.

When the sun started to climb above the Eastern horizon, she hurried to Mātavi's house to recount all that she had seen and heard. As Sutamati told her all these things in great detail, Mātavi was left speechless and bewildered. Particularly the news that Maṇimēkalai had been carried away to Maṇipallavam, pained her greatly.

5

Maṇimēkalai on Maṇipallavam

Meanwhile Maṇimēkalai, after being carried to Maṇipallavam in a trance, slowly came to her senses. When she opened her eyes, she found herself in entirely new surroundings, and could not make out where she was. Wherever she looked, she could only see rolling dunes of white sand.

From the roaring of the waves, she guessed that she was near a beach. The presence of laurel trees and the cackling of the cranes confirmed her guess. Still she thought that she was in another corner of the Uvavaṉam gardens. But when she realized that Sutamati was no longer close by, she began to worry.

"Where are you, Sutamati?" she cried. "Where have you gone? Why have you deserted me? When you left me, it was evening. Now I can see the sun just rising above the Eastern horizon. My mother will be very worried about me. How can I return to her without you? Could it be that the strange woman whom I saw talking to you has carried you away?"

Maṇimēkalai's mind was troubled by all kinds of frightening thoughts, but she soon steadied herself and began to explore the place in which she found herself, in the hope of finding Sutamati somewhere in the vicinity.

As she walked on, she realized that she was in an altogether unfamiliar place. She could only conclude that she had been kidnapped and taken there by someone with evil intentions. Her plaited hair was blown about by the wind, which made her look dishevelled and unkempt.

Thoughts about the fate of Sutamati and fears about her mother's peace of mind tormented her. For a moment, there passed through her mind the fleeting memory of the way her father Kōvalaṉ had met his death in Maturai at the hands of the Pāṇḍiyaṉ king.

The Holy Seat of the Buddha

Suddenly there appeared before her a raised platform glittering with jewels known as the Holy Seat (*taruma āsaṉam*), where the Lord Buddha sat to give instruction to his followers. At this sight Maṇimēkalai spontaneously joined her hands together in worship. Tears of happiness filled her eyes. She fell to the ground like a flash of lightning from the sky, and then rose reverently to her feet.

Drying her tears, slowly Maṇimēkalai regained her poise. Her heart became lighter and her mind clearer. Her doubts dissolved and her power of concentration returned. As she felt this change taking place within her, Maṇimēkalā Teyvam appeared before her like a bolt from the blue.

The goddess first bowed low before the Buddha's Holy Seat, and then fell to the ground in worship. When the goddess had risen to her feet, Maṇimēkalai realized who the strange lady was and fell down before her. First she thanked the goddess for revealing to her the details of her previous birth. Then, unable to contain her anxiety, Maṇimēkalai asked the goddess, "Where is he who was my husband?"

Maṇimēkalai's previous birth

"My dear Maṇimēkalai," the goddess began, "as you have now realized, your husband in your previous birth was called Rākulaṉ. One day when you and he were playing a game together, you went into a sulk. Since your husband loved you very dearly, he did everything possible to please you and to bring you out of your sulk. But you were adamant, and would not be mollified.

"At that moment a celestial being called Sādhu Chakkaraṉ came down from the sky and stood before you. At once your mood changed and you fell down before the celestial visitor, who was a powerful sage.

"Your husband took offence at the undue respect you paid to this stranger, and he demanded that you tell him who the visitor was. When you heard your husband's rough words, you trembled in alarm that he had suspected you, without realizing who that great celestial being was.

"You gently placed your hand over your husband's lips, politely scolded him for his rudeness, and made him too bow down before the Sādhu. You spoke kind words to the sage and asked him to have a meal with you. The sage agreed, and you both served him food with fitting reverence.

"Because of your loving kindness you have been enabled to learn of your past, and to gain freedom from rebirth. It is your previous husband Rākulaṉ who has now been reborn as Utayakumaraṉ. That is why he is in the toils of such passionate desire to win you. It is your past relationship as man and wife that is making him pursue you so relentlessly, and it is the same connection from the past which makes you find him so attractive. Your name in that previous birth was Lakshmi. I have brought you here specially to tell you all these things about your past.

"Now dear Lakshmi, I will tell you something more. In that birth, you had two sisters, one called Tārai, the other Vīrai. They were both married to Tuchayaṉ, the king of Aṅka Nāḍu."

Maṇimēkalai was amazed to hear this, and listened with careful attention. After a brief pause, Maṇimēkalā Teyvam revealed to her more of her past history.

The Lotus Foot mountain

"One day king Tuchayaṉ, your sisters' husband, was far away in the mountains," the goddess continued. "As he was enjoying the beauty of nature, he chanced to meet Aṟavaṇa Aḍikaḷ. Not recognizing that great Buddhist saint, he politely asked him who he was and what had brought him there. Although the saint was so famous, he was not offended by the king's innocent question. On the contrary, he replied with all humility.

" 'There was a great soul called Buddha,' said the sage, 'who wished that all beings should enjoy life free from disease, ignorance, poverty and oppression. So he climbed this mountain and from its summit he preached words of eternal truth and wisdom. He continued preaching in that way for months on end. As a result, the spot where he stood to preach became marked with the impression of his two lotus feet. Because of those foot prints, this mountain has earned the name Lotus Foot Mountain.

" 'I am now returning home after worshipping the marks of the Lord Buddha's lotus feet on its summit. If you visit the mountain top and gain sight of those foot marks, you will be richly blesssed.' With these words Aṟavaṇa Aḍikaḷ took leave of the king and went his way.

"As instructed by Aṟavaṇa Aḍikaḷ, king Tuchayaṉ and his two wives climbed the mountain and worshipped the lotus feet of the Buddha on its summit. Because of the merit gained by that deed, Tārai and Vīrai came back to earth in their next lives as Mātavi and Sutamati, and now they are greatly concerned about your welfare."

Maṇimēkalai learns some mantras

In this way Maṇimēkalai learned of her past connection with Mātavi and Sutamati. The goddess then went on to advise Maṇimēkalai on what tasks she should next undertake:

"Now you have learnt something of your past history," she continued. "Next you have to learn about the teachings of other religions. In doing so, you should particularly focus on the good things about those religions. If the leaders of such rival religions shy away from teaching you their doctrines on the excuse that you are too young, then it may become necessary for you to change your appearance. To enable you to take on such a disguise, I will teach you the appropriate mantra.

"You should realize that knowledge of religions is of no use to people unless it helps them to get rid of their sufferings, such as poverty, hunger and ignorance. There is no point in teaching people religious doctrines that might help them reach heaven, if they are hungry and miserable as a result.

"Hunger is the most cruel thing of all. Therefore you must take it as your first duty to assuage the terrible hunger of the masses. I will tell you a mantra which if properly chanted will enable you to remove their hunger."

So the goddess taught Maṇimēkalai the mantras which would enable her to assuage the hunger of the people, to assume any disguise at will, and to fly invisibly through the air. Then she took her leave.

Tīvatilakai meets Maṇimēkalai

As a result of her meeting with Maṇimēkalā Teyvam, and by learning from her some useful mantras, Maṇimēkalai's fears about Utayakumaraṉ were relieved. But still looking dejected, she continued to walk around the island of Maṇipallavam, to see the lie of the land, and to enjoy its wild flowers and animals.

At this moment another goddess came on the scene, called Tīvatilakai. Seeing Maṇimēkalai in such a pensive mood, Tīvatilakai wanted to know who she was and what had brought her to the island. So she approached Maṇimēkalai and asked her why she had come to such a lonely place and what it was that was tormenting her so.

"I do not know who you are and why you have come," said Maṇimēkalai. "But you look like someone whom I can trust and that gives me hope. Because you ask me with genuine concern, I will tell you who I am.

"My name is Maṇimēkalai. In my previous birth I was lucky enough to be the wife of a king called Rākulaṉ. Maṇimēkalā Teyvam brought me here, and granted me enlightenment. It was by her grace that I was able to see the Buddha's Holy Seat. As a result of my worshipping here, I learnt of my previous birth.

"Now that I have told you who I am, would you please tell me who you are," asked Maṇimēkalai politely.

Maṇimēkalai receives a magic bowl

When Maṇimēkalai told her how she had received the grace of Maṇimēkalā Teyvam, Tīvatilakai realized that the young woman she was speaking to must be a deserving person; so she began to tell Maṇimēkalai about herself.

"Next to Maṇipallavam, where we are now," she said, "there is a larger island called Ratna Tīvu, and on it there is a mountain range called Samanta Kūḍam. On its highest point can be seen the foot prints of the Lord Buddha. Having worshipped the foot prints there, I came to this island sometime ago.

"A strange attachment to this place made me forget everything, and I took this island as my permanent home. Indra, the god of the heavens, ordained that I should stand guard before the Buddha's seat, and so I spend my life here. My name is Tīvatilakai.

"Those who are privileged to worship the Lord Buddha and to follow his teaching will be blessed in this life and will attain everything they desire," Tīvatilakai continued. "They will also develop the power of knowing their previous births. Having come here and worshipped the Buddha's seat, you have learnt about your past. You are really blessed.

"In front of this Holy Seat, you will see a sacred tank called Kōmuki. On the day of the full moon in the month Vaikāsi, which is the birthday of the Lord Buddha, there will emerge from that tank a wondrous bowl called Amuta Surabi. That bowl can supply food to any number of people without ever running out. Today is the day of the full moon. If you need to know any more about this bowl," she concluded, "Please ask Aṟavaṇa Aḍikaḷ."

Maṇimēkalai was very pleased to have met Tīvatilakai and to have gathered all this information. She fell down before the Buddha's seat in adoration once more and then rose to her feet. Maṇimēkalai and Tīvatilakai then proceeded together to Kōmuki, the sacred tank. When they reached its brink, Maṇimēkalai stood there reverently in prayer, forgetting herself.

Suddenly in the middle of the tank ripples appeared, and the wondrous bowl Amuta Surabi emerged from the water. It travelled in the air towards Maṇimēkalai, who was standing awestruck. When it came within her reach, involuntarily she stretched out her hands to receive it. Her joy knew no bounds.

Having thus received the bowl, Maṇimēkalai went straight to the Holy Seat and offered homage. Tears of ecstasy filled her eyes and rolled down her cheeks. Tīvatilakai who was patiently watching all this, congratulated Maṇimēkalai on her good fortune and began to speak further about the horrors of hunger and thirst.

"Hunger is a dangerous and terrible condition," she said. "It is the root cause for many of the sins and evils of the world. Persistent hunger and the lack of the means to avert it will ruin everything.

"Hunger will destroy one's sense of shame and honour. It will cloud the desire for learning. It will kill the sense of generosity. It will bring about forgetfulness, and wipe out the memory of all that one has ever learnt. It will weaken the ability to persevere. It will even kill the desire for bodily pleasure. Since such are the effects of hunger, every effort should be made to eliminate it, if a country is to be peaceful and happy."

Tīvatilakai's advice gave Maṇimēkalai new understanding of the terrible plight of those who suffer from hunger. Accordingly, she decided to put Amuta Surabi to good use by bringing light and life to the thousands of hungry people in the world.

Mātavi's anxiety

While all these wonderful things were happening to Maṇimēkalai at Maṇipallavam, at Pūmpukār Mātavi was growing increasingly anxious that her daughter had not returned at the end of the seven days as foretold by Maṇimēkalā Teyvam. Mātavi visited the Buddhist temple, and prayed for Maṇimēkalai's safe return.

Even as Mātavi was worrying at Pūmpukār, at Mannṇipallavam Tīvatilakai was urging Maṇimēkalai to leave for Pūmpukār without delay. So Maṇimēkalai thanked Tīvatilakai profusely, and solemnly worshipped at the Buddha's seat once more. Then, holding the sacred bowl firmly in her hand, and reciting the magic formula, Maṇimēkalai took off from the ground and rose swiftly into the sky.

Mātavi and Sutamati were still waiting anxiously, when to their utter astonishment Maṇimēkalai descended from the sky and stood before them. They embraced her passionately and breathed a great sigh of relief.

After an exchange of pleasantries, Mātavi sensed that Maṇimēkalai had been transformed and become a totally new person. Her measured words showed that she had attained enlightenment. Since Mātavi and Sutamati knew nothing of their previous births, Maṇimēkalai told them all she had learnt about their past lives while they listened in silent amazement.

"Dear daughters of Ravivaṉmaṉ, in your previous birth you both were my sisters. Our father was Ravivaṉmaṉ and our mother was Amutapati. My present mother Mātavi's name was Tārai. Sutamati's name was Vīrai and my name was Lakshmi. In your previous birth you both were the wives of Tuchayaṉ.

"In this birth, you have now become my mother and stepmother. I bow before you. Now I strongly urge you to go and meet Aṟavaṇa Aḍikaḷ, who will be able to help you. None of us need remain in this cycle of birth and rebirth any longer. We have to find a way to gain release, for it is only through ceasing to be reborn that we can attain the bliss of *nirvana*.

"Meanwhile, please take a look at this bowl. It is called Amuta Surabi, and it can satisfy the hunger of millions of people. However much food you take from it, it will never run out. The more you take from it, the more it gives. The supply it contains is truly inexhaustible. Once upon a time it was in the possession of a great soul called Āputtiraṉ. Please pay homage to this divine bowl." Obediently Mātavi and Sutamati fell to the ground in homage before the bowl, then rose to their feet.

Aṟavaṇa Aḍikaḷ's revelation

Maṇimēkalai was impatient to meet Aṟavaṇa Aḍikaḷ, so together with Mātavi and Sutamati she went to the Buddha temple to look for him. When they came into his presence, they made obeisance before him.

Aṟavaṇa Aḍikaḷ looked very weak, though he was still alert in mind. Maṇimēkalai told him how she had gone to Uvavaṉam, how she was rescued from there by Maṇimēkalā Teyvam and taken to Maṇipallavam, how she had found enlightenment on that island, and how finally she had come to possess Amuta Surabi.

Aṟavaṇa Aḍikaḷ was overjoyed to hear all this, so as suggested by Maṇimēkalā Teyvam, Maṇimēkalai went on to ask the sage to tell them the past history of Tārai and Vīrai. Maṇimēkalai also asked the sage if he could tell them something more about the divine bowl, Amuta Surabi. Aṟavaṇa Aḍikaḷ was greatly impressed by Maṇimēkalai, so he told her all that she wanted to know.

"There is a mountain called Lotus Feet Mountain," he began. "One day I went to that mountain to worship the imprint of the feet of the Lord Buddha, which is on its summit. On my way home from there, I met king Tuchayaṉ in a garden, and enquired after his two wives. He started to weep and wail, which puzzled me greatly. I allowed him to cry for a while, so that his sorrow might be eased. Then I gently urged him to tell me the cause of his deep sadness.

"Tuchayaṉ told me that his older wife Tārai was killed by a wild elephant. Unable to bear her loss, his younger wife Vīrai committed suicide by throwing herself down from the roof of their house. When I heard this sad story, I was overcome by grief, and did not know how to comfort him. I acknowledged that such things were beyond human understanding, and could only be explained in terms of destiny".

Aṟavaṇa Aḍikaḷ finished the story and looked at Mātavi and Sutamati. They were overcome by amazement.

"Now," Aṟavaṇa Aḍikaḷ continued, "I see those two ladies in front of me. Just as in a play one actor can take on many parts, so both of you have now taken on new roles."

When he had finished telling them about the fate of Tārai and Vīrai, Aṟavaṇa Aḍikaḷ began to speak in glowing terms about Maṇimēkalā Teyvam.

"My dear Maṇimēkalai," he continued, "You are blessed indeed to have received the grace of Maṇimēkalā Teyvam! In the coming days you are going to perform many miracles in this country. Only after performing all those miracles will you be able to understand the advice that I am now going to give you.

"Your companions Mātavi and Sutamati will go to worship at the Lotus Feet Mountain, and there they will receive the blessing of the Lord Buddha. Then they will be released from all bonds and will attain eternal bliss.

"The miraculous bowl which you have found is able to relieve the hunger not only of earthly beings, but of heavenly beings as well. You may be sure that satisfying their hunger will be the best of all acts of charity. May you serve humanity and rid the country of poverty with all its attendant misery!"

Maṇimēkalai thanked Aṟavaṇa Aḍikaḷ for his blessing, and promised that she would try to live up to his expectations. Then she asked him to tell her the story of Āputtiraṉ who had passed on to her the wonderful bowl, Amuta Surabi. So Aṟavaṇa Aḍikaḷ began to tell Maṇimēkalai that story too.

6

The story of Āputtiraṉ

In answer to Maṇimēkalai's request, this is the story that Aṟavaṇa Aḍikaḷ told:

In the city of Vāranāsi, there lived a Brahmin called Apañchikaṉ with his wife, Sāli. By an unfortunate accident, Sāli committed a sin against her marriage vows. To atone for that sin, she undertook a pilgrimage to various shrines in the South of the country. At that time she was pregnant with a child conceived out of wedlock.

In the course of her pilgrimage she reached the city of Koṟkai in the Pāṇḍiya country. As the time was near for her baby to be born, she could not travel any further, but took refuge in a deserted shed in the woods. There, unassisted by anyone, she gave birth to a baby boy. Since her husband was not the father of the child, she reluctantly decided to abandon it, and went on her way leaving it to its fate.

The abandoned child lay there in the shed crying for milk, until a cow, which was grazing nearby, heard its cry and came to its rescue. The cow settled down beside the baby and fed it with milk from its own udder.

When the child's hunger was satisfied, the cow remained close by, grazing as before. It hoped that some humans would come along and take charge of the baby. From time to time the cow went to the child and suckled it, so that there was no need for it to cry. At night the cow sat close by and kept watch. In this way, seven days passed, with the cow performing its motherly duty of feeding the human child.

On the eighth day, a Brahmin called Iḷam Pūti chanced to pass that way with his wife, at the very moment when the cow was suckling the baby. Pūti was astonished at the sight, and having no children of his own, he concluded that God had at last shown mercy on him, by allowing him to find an abandoned child to adopt as his own. So he picked up the child with gratitude and gave it to his wife to look after. The child held on to her tightly, shedding tears of joy. The cow too was happy that the baby had at last been taken into the care of a human couple.

As the couple walked off with the baby, the cow followed for some distance. Finally, assured that the baby was in safe hands, the cow retraced its steps. Nevertheless it was still angry that after giving birth the mother had abandoned her own child in that lonely wood.

Since the baby had been fed by a cow, the couple decided to call him Āputtiraṉ, which means the child of the cow. Although the couple did not know to which caste the child belonged, they brought him up as a Brahmin. Āputtiraṉ showed himself to be an intelligent child, and grew up to master all the religious texts and many other subjects besides. So he won the respect of the community for his learning.

As Āputtiraṉ's family were Brahmins, they used to perform religious rituals to win the favour of the gods. As part of those rituals, they would kill animals to offer as sacrifices. Āputtiraṉ hated the idea of killing animals and decided that he would work to have that cruel practice forbidden.

Āputtiraṉ rebels

One day Āputtiraṉ visited the house of a Brahmin relative. There, tied to a post, he saw a cow that was to be sacrificed on the following day. The sight pained him greatly, and he decided by hook or by crook to free the animal. So that night he went to his relative's house, furtively untied the cow and started to drive it away.

By chance at that very moment the owner of the cow woke up. When he got up and looked around, he found the cow was missing. At once he raised a hue and cry and alerted the neighbourhood. With a few other Brahmins, he looked around for clues, and soon spotted fresh hoof marks on the road which showed that the cow had just recently passed that way.

They quickly caught up with Āputtiraṉ and gave him a good beating. When the cow saw the boy being punished like that, it went wild. It butted and gored the Brahmins, and having wrought havoc among them, it vanished from their sight.

The Brahmins then tied Āputtiraṉ's hands and took him to the house of the cow's owner. Undeterred by the beating he had been given, Āputtiraṉ challenged the Brahmins' practice of killing animals at their so-called Vedic sacrifices.

"What good could it possibly do to take the life of an innocent animal?" he asked. "Why do you not realize that to refrain from wantonly slaughtering an animal, and then to refrain from eating its flesh, is far superior to performing a thousand burnt offerings for the delight of the celestials?"

The Brahmins could give the boy no satisfactory answer. All they could do was to speak slightingly to him. One of them taunted him, saying, "How can the son of a cow know the ins and outs of Vedic rites and rituals?"

Āputtiraṉ was himself equally learned in the scriptures; so on hearing these remarks, he was stung to the quick, and began to quote chapter and verse from the ancient texts.

"Listen to me, you Brahmins," replied Āputtiraṉ, "You consider Asalaṉ, Siruṅki, Viriṅki and Kēsakampaḷaṉ all to be great sages, don't you? Well, in case you did not know, let me tell you something about them.

"Asalaṉ is the son of a cow; Siruṅki is the son of a deer; Viriṅki is the son of a tigress; and Kēsakampaḷaṉ is the son of a fox. If those sages are worthy of your veneration, how can you speak ill of my birth? Anyway, how can you be sure that my father was an animal?"

At this, the Brahmins were lost for words. Unable to give any reply, one of them began to speak ill of the character of Āputtiraṉ's mother.

"What is the point of talking to this fellow who does not even know who his mother was?" he asked. "Her name was Sāli. She misbehaved with a man who was not her husband. To atone for her sin, she came South on a pilgrimage all the way from Vāranāsi to Kaṉṉiyākumari. I happened to meet her on her way, and she told me everything.

"This fellow is the son of that shameless woman. He was later picked up by Iḷam Pūti, who told me that the boy was looked after by a cow until he and his wife rescued him. The fellow does not know his own father either. This is the upstart who is now quoting to us chapter and verse from the Vedas!"

The Brahmins silenced

When the Brahmin spoke so disrespectfully of Āputtiraṉ's origin, other Brahmins also were emboldened to hurl abuse at him. But Āputtiraṉ remained unruffled through it all, and replied coolly:

"Gentlemen!" said Āputtiraṉ. "As you have now revealed, my mother walked all the way from Vāranāsi to Kaṉṉiyākumari on pilgrimage. She wanted to atone for her involuntary sin by bathing at the place where the three seas meet. Does she not deserve to be praised for her sincerity of purpose?

"Now let me ask you again, gentlemen. Do you by any chance know the parentage of Vasiṭṭar and Akattiyar? No, no one knows, nor do they know who their mothers were either. Did you know that Tilōttamai was a celestial prostitute? She earned her living through dancing and prostitution.

"Although Vasiṭṭar and Akattiyar are the sons of a prostitute, they are counted worthy to receive your veneration. If children of such dubious origin can be venerated, how dare you speak ill of my mother, who never intentionally committed any sin at all?"

Iḷam Pūti disowns his son

When they heard this, the Brahmins were tongue-tied and hung their heads in shame. Then they slunk away and reported to Iḷam Pūti what they had learnt about Āputtiraṉ's parents, and how the young man had spoken disrespectfully to them. This made Iḷam Pūti furious, and he decided to disown Āputtiraṉ as an outcaste. So when his adopted son came home, Pūti shut the door in his face.

Āputtiraṉ took no offence at this treatment, but told his step-parents that he would remain eternally grateful to them for all that they had done for him. So saying, he made obeisance before them for the last time, and took his leave.

From that time on, Āputtiraṉ decided to lead the life of a wandering beggar with a bowl in his hand. The Brahmins of the town were so influential that they prevailed on all the other householders not to give him any alms. Instead of food, they put rubbish and pebbles in his bowl. So he moved out of that town and went South to the city of Maturai. There he lived a contented life by begging.

He shared most of what he received as alms with others in the same situation as himself, particularly with orphans, the old, the deaf, the blind, and the lame. In this way, he begged not only for himself but also for all those who were weak and oppressed in society. He derived great pleasure from seeing a smile dawn on the faces of those who were less fortunate than himself.

Āputtiran̲ in a quandary

In this way, Āputtiran̲ took upon himself the duty of helping the needy by means of his begging bowl. So it happened that one night while he was resting in a house of refuge for the needy, some strangers approached him and said that they were tormented with hunger. They asked him to give them something to eat, for they had heard of his generosity and had high hopes that he would find a way to help them.

That night Āputtiran̲ did not have any food left, but still he did not have the heart to say "no" and to turn them away. He wondered whether there might be some householder whom he could disturb at that hour of the night to beg for food, but he could not think of anyone.

So he prayed to God and begged that he be shown a way to render timely help to the distressed strangers who were waiting expectantly. Āputtiraṉ could not bear the thought that he could do nothing for them, and tears rolled down his cheeks.

The magic bowl

While Āputtiraṉ was caught in this dilemma, there appeared before him a celestial being called Sintātēvi with a bowl in her hand that was always full of food. The name of the bowl was Amuta Surabi. She smiled at the sorrowing Āputtiraṉ, showed him the bowl, and said:-

"Do not worry any more, my son. You may keep this bowl as your own. There is enough food in it for all your needs. You will always find it full, and it will never run out. Even if you had to feed the whole country, there would be enough food in it. So carry on your selfless service of relieving the misery of the poor. This bowl is yours forever. Please take it; it is my gift to you."

Unable to believe what he heard, Āputtiraṉ fell down before Sintātēvi and thankfully took the bowl from her hand. Wishing him well, Sintātēvi then vanished into thin air.

The hungry people who were waiting for Āputtiraṉ to help them were amazed. Āputtiraṉ was now able joyfully to call them together and to satisfy their hunger. Delighted with this wonderful gift, Āputtiraṉ used it to continue his service to the hungry. Even the animals and birds were not left out; they came flocking round him like pets.

Indra comes on the scene

The news that Āputtiraṉ had been given a divine bowl capable of feeding the entire world spread far and wide. Indra, the god of the heavens, also heard that Āputtiraṉ was busily engaged in this valuable service; so at once he came down to earth to bestow his blessing upon him:-

"Āputtiraṉ!" he began, "I am Indra, the god of the heavens. All men sing the praises of the great service which you are performing. If you are expecting some reward for what you do, whatever that reward may be, I will readily grant it to you. You have only to ask."

Hearing these words, Āputtiraṉ laughed. He believed that heaven has nothing which is not available here below, and that the celestial beings exist only to reap the benefit of the meritorious deeds performed by human beings on earth. With that idea in mind, Āputtiraṉ replied to Indra's offer.

"Hail, chief of the gods!" he said, "I bow in gratitude before you for your kind words. However, I have a question for you.

"Can you tell me in what way your heaven is superior to this earthly realm? Is it not correct to say that it is only on earth that doers of good deeds are to be found? Is it not here on earth that people perform penances and delight to offer hospitality to strangers? Are such virtuous people to be found in heaven?

"Amuta Surabi alone is enough for me. With it I can befriend the needy and satisfy their hunger. I am not clear what other reward you could give me. What exactly have you in mind?"

Indra was puzzled by Āputtiraṉ's words, for he never dreamed that he would answer him with such boldness. So he began to reflect.

"This fellow derives pleasure and peace of mind from the smile of those whom he is able to feed," he thought. "That is why he says that he wants nothing else, and has no need for any further reward. How can I bring him to my feet? What if I create a situation in which nobody will come to him to beg? If no one comes to him, how can he experience the contentment which he now enjoys?

"This is what I shall do: I will make the land so abundant in all manner of plenty that there will be no need for anyone to beg. If I do that, Āputtiraṉ will not be able to show such boldness."

Indra at once began to give effect to his plan. The country which had not seen a drop of rain for more than twelve years began to receive plentiful rain at regular intervals, until there was an abundant supply of vegetables and crops of every kind. As a result, everyone had enough and no one needed to depend on anyone else for their livelihood. Moreover, nobody looked to Āputtiraṉ for help, nor was there any need for all the supply that Amuta Surabi had to offer.

Āputtiraṉ is marooned

When he realized that there was no longer any need for Amuta Surabi, Āputtiraṉ decided to leave the Pāṇḍiya country and move to another place where he could be of some use.

So he travelled from place to place constantly asking those he met whether they were in need of food. Those who heard him going on like this wondered whether he was mad. However, unmindful of what anyone said, Āputtiraṉ continued to travel around looking for needy people to help.

One day Āputtiraṉ heard in the market place that the people of the country called Chāvakam were starving as the result of a serious drought. Moved by a desire to help the people of that land, Āputtiraṉ set sail across the sea. While on his way, in mid-ocean a severe storm blew up which forced the captain of the ship to anchor off the shore of the island of Maṇipallavam. There he ordered all the passengers to disembark.

Accordingly, with everyone else Āputtiraṉ landed on the island, and there decided to take a walk round to see all that there was to see. He assumed that the stormy weather would continue for some days, so that it would be a while before the captain would be able to resume the voyage.

However, when Āputtiraṉ returned to the shore that evening, he found that the captain had already put to sea, mistakenly believing that everyone had re-embarked. So Āputtiraṉ was effectively marooned on the uninhabited island of Maṇipallavam.

What could he do in such a desolate place, he wondered, and what use to him now was his wonderful bowl, Amuta Surabi. So in deep despair, he began to walk aimlessly around.

Āputtiraṉ discards Amuta Surabi

As he walked, he came across the tank called Kōmuki, and the sight of it brought a strange thought to his mind. It occurred to him to throw Amuta Surabi into the tank in the hope that someone in the future would find it, and that it might be of use to them. Looking tenderly at the bowl, he said:

"My beloved Amuta Surabi! You have been so useful to me and to thousands of hungry people all this time. Now I am marooned on an island where I have no further use for you.

"So I am now going to drop you into the water of this tank with the humble request that you come to the surface of the water once every year. Then if you chance to see anyone who in your opinion could put you to good use, entrust yourself to their keeping and do even more service for them than you have done for me."

With these words, Āputtiraṉ gently dropped the bowl into the tank and said goodbye to it with tears. He had never been the slave of attachment to anything in life, and now he lost even the little desire that he had.

Just as he was considering fasting to the point of death, in the nick of time Aṟavaṇa Aḍikaḷ arrived on the scene. When the sage heard the story of Āputtiraṉ and saw that he was now seriously thinking of ending his life, he tried his best to persuade him to change his mind. But Āputtiraṉ would not listen, and carried out the drastic decision to end his life there on the island of Maṇipallavam.

Āputtiraṉ is reborn

By the decree of the gods, the divine cow which had suckled Āputtiraṉ when he was lying forsaken by his mother as an infant in the woods, came to a mountain called Tavalamalai in the same Chāvaka country. At that time a great sage called Maṇmukaṉ had settled on the top of that mountain and was performing severe penances there.

When the cow reached the place where the sage was, she quietly stood by his side. The sage seemed pleased that the cow had come, and blessed her. He realized that the cow would remain there and in due course give birth to a human child who would perform miraculous deeds for the benefit of humanity. On the full moon day of the month of Vaikāsi, the divine cow did indeed give birth to a baby boy.

On that very day in Pūmpukār, the people of Chakkaravāḷa Kōṭṭam saw many signs and omens.

According to popular belief, those omens resembled the ones which had appeared on the day when the Lord Buddha was born. Amazed by those unusual signs, the gods of Chakkaravāḷa Kōṭṭam approached Kantil Pāvai, the statuette attached to the pillar in the Sampāpati temple, and asked for an explanation of their meaning.

Kantil Pāvai explained to them that Āputtiraṉ who had fasted to death on the island of Maṇipallavam some years previously, had now been born again as a human child in the womb of a cow in the Chāvaka country.

Chāvakam was awash with the news about Āputtiraṉ's miraculous birth to the divine cow in the hermitage of the sage Maṇmukaṉ. Būmi Chandran, the king of Chāvakam, had no heir; so when he heard the news, he approached the sage and expressed his desire to adopt the cow's child as a royal prince.

The sage spoke highly of the qualities of the child, and commended him as fit to become heir to the throne. Accordingly Būmi Chandran adopted the child, and gave him the name Puṇṇiyarāsaṉ. The child grew up, and as foretold became king of that land. In this way, Āputtiraṉ who had fasted to death on Maṇipallavam island was reborn and became the king of Chāvakam.

So at last Aṟavaṇa Aḍikaḷ brought the story of Āputtiraṉ to an end. Then he turned to Maṇimēkalai and laid upon her a new task. "Since poverty and famine are now killing the people of Chāvakam in their thousands," he said, "you must now go there with Amuta Surabi to bring them relief."

Filled with wonder at this story, Maṇimēkalai thanked Aṟavaṇa Aḍikaḷ for his words, and set about making plans to go to Chāvakam as he had commanded, together with her mother Mātavi and her friend Sutamati.

7

Maṇimēkalai puts Amuta Surabi to use

When Amuta Surabi first came into the hands of Maṇimēkalai at the Kōmuki tank, she was instructed that for the bowl to become active, the first alms she received should be from a woman of unblemished virtue. So now Maṇimēkalai dressed herself as a Buddhist nun and walked along the streets of Pūmpukār with the bowl in her hand begging.

When the people of the city saw her dressed as a nun, they gathered round with curiosity. "Is this not the girl who ran away when prince Utayakumara<u>n</u> tried to woo her?" asked one woman. "How is it that she has now come like this, wearing the garb of a nun?" remarked another.

When Maṇimēkalai declared before them all that the first person to fill her bowl must be someone of outstanding virtue, a woman called Kāya Chaṇḍikai stepped forward from the crowd. She recommended to Maṇimēkalai another woman called Ātirai as a possible candidate for this role, and directed Maṇimēkalai to her house. So Maṇimēkalai duly went off to meet her.

By the time that Maṇimēkalai reached her house, Ātirai had already heard about her. So she quickly came to the door, walked reverently around the visitor and fell to the ground before her.

On hearing the purpose of Maṇimēkalai's visit, Ātirai gladly filled the bowl with rice and blessed her with long life and success in her mission. No sooner had Ātirai filled the bowl than it began to overflow with rice. This made Maṇimēkalai confident that Amuta Surabi would now be able to satisfy the hunger of the people.

8

The story of Ātirai

Struck by Ātirai's gentle and simple manner, Maṇimēkalai at once took a liking to her. So, wishing to know more about her, she asked Kāya Chaṇḍikai to tell her about Ātirai's background.

"Ātirai is a woman of impeccable virtue," replied Kāya Chaṇḍikai. "She is married to a man called Chātuvaṉ of whom the same could not be said. He associated with loose women and lost all his wealth. Having been reduced to poverty, he decided to go abroad in an attempt to recover his lost riches. Accordingly, along with other enterprising merchants he set sail in a ship for distant lands.

"In mid-ocean, the ship was struck by a cyclone and sank, drowning many of those on board. However, Chātuvaṉ was a great swimmer, and managed to swim ashore on an island inhabited by a tribe called the Nāgas.

"Unbeknown to Chātuvaṉ, some of his companions also survived the shipwreck, and returned to Maturai. When the news of the wreck reached the ears of Ātirai, she approached one of the survivors and asked him whether he had any news of Chātuvaṉ. He told her that most of the passengers had drowned, and so it was more than likely that Chātuvaṉ too was dead.

"Ātirai was deeply saddend by this news, and decided to commit suicide by casting herself into a fire. As she was about to carry out her plan, she heard a strange voice from heaven addressing her.

"The voice told her that Chātuvaṉ had survived the shipwreck, that he was safe on a distant island, and that he would return to her soon. Overjoyed at this news, Ātirai changed her mind about committing suicide and began to lead a life of service to her community.

"After he had swum ashore safely, Chātuvaṉ was exhausted by the heat and tormented by hunger. So he sat down under a shady coconut tree and fell asleep.

"A team of Nāga hunters chanced to pass by the spot where he was resting. When they saw him, they were glad to have found their food for the day. So they began shouting and singing their tribal songs. Startled by the noise, Chātuvaṉ woke up to see a group of unkempt men armed with bows and arrows surrounding him.

"Unperturbed by the fierce appearance of the hunters, Chātuvaṉ spoke to them in their own tongue. They were pleased that a fair-skinned foreigner could speak their crude language, and took him to their leader. Chātuvaṉ spoke respectfully to the Nāga leader and explained to him how he had come to land on their island.

"The Nāga leader ordered his men to look after their guest well, and to provide him with food, wine and women. Chātuvaṉ ate such of the food as was vegetarian, but declined the offer of wine and women. He told the Nāga leader that wine and women cannot give lasting peace and pleasure, and that the Nāga people too should avoid eating meat, drinking wine, and indulging in sexual orgies.

"Surprised at this advice, his host asked Chātuvaṉ how one could find true peace. In reply, Chātuvaṉ explained to him the teachings of the Buddha, and the Nāga leader appeared convinced by Chātuvaṉ's advice.

"After spending a couple of days on the island, Chātuvaṉ expressed the desire to return to his own country. So the Nāga leader organized a ship to carry him back to Maturai, laden with sandal wood, elephant tusks and akil wood. When Chātuvaṉ reached home safely, he rejoined his wife Ātirai and turned over a new leaf in life. Now they are an ideal couple, and that," concluded Kāya Chaṇḍikai, "is the story of Ātirai."

The healing of Kāya Chaṇḍikai

Now for twelve years as the result of a curse, Kāya Chaṇḍikai had been suffering from a strange and distressing illness which made her insatiably hungry the whole time.

So she now approached Maṇimēkalai and confided to her that not only had she been suffering from this awful disease, but she was also sunk in unremitting depression. She begged Maṇimēkalai to give her some food from her bowl to appease her terrible hunger. In response to this appeal, Maṇimēkalai scooped out a ball of rice and gave it to her.

As soon as she had swallowed the rice, Kāya Chaṇḍikai was miraculously freed from the curse and cured of her long-standing illness. Curious to know how Kāya Chaṇḍikai had come to be cursed in that way, Maṇimēkalai asked her how it had happened. So Kāya Chaṇḍikai told Maṇimēkalai her story:

"I come from the world of the lesser gods, called Kāñciṉapuram. One day, my husband and I left our world and came down to this earth to enjoy the beautiful scenery of the Potikai hills. While we were staying in that region, one day we came to the bank of a rushing mountain stream.

"At the same time a sage came by who introduced himself as Viruchikaṉ. He had a large jambo fruit in his hand, wrapped in teak leaves. He put the fruit on the ground and went to the river bank to bathe. Before entering the water, he asked us casually to keep watch on the fruit, to which we gladly agreed.

"The sage stayed a long time in the water, and eventually I grew tired of sitting there and stood up to stretch my legs. As I got up and walked a few steps, I quite forgot that the jambo fruit was lying close by. Accidentally I trod on it and crushed it to pulp.

"I felt very distressed at this, and did not know what to do. When the sage returned and found his fruit reduced to pulp, he flew into a rage. I tried to apologize and explain, but I could not get a word in edgeways.

"'This is a miraculous fruit,' he stormed. 'It comes from a particular tree which bears only one fruit, and that too only once in twelve years. Moreover, I eat only once in twelve years, and I eat nothng except this one fruit. By trampling on it, you have deprived me of my only food, and condemned me to starvation for another twelve years.

" 'By your carelessness, you have earned my curse: from this moment you will forget the mantra which has enabled you to travel through the sky; you will also instantly be struck by a disease which will cause you to be tormented by insatiable hunger. That will last for twelve years. Only when I eat another fruit like this in twelve years' time will you be rid of this terrible illness.'

"I was shattered by what he had said. Falling at his feet, I begged the sage to take back the curse, but he refused to relent and went on his way.

"Even before the sage left, I began to feel the pangs of hunger, which made me feel miserable. I tried to remember the mantra to travel through the sky, but I could not. So there was no way that I could return to my own world of the demigods.

"My husband too was helpless. He could not take me back with him, nor could he cure me of the illness. So he advised me to come here to Kāviri Pūmpaṭṭiṉam, where I began a new life on my own. My husband visits me every year during the Indra festival."

Kāya Chaṇḍikai finished her story with a sigh of relief, overjoyed to be freed at last from the curse and cured of her illness. Now all she wanted was for Maṇimēkalai to visit the house called Ulaka Aṟavi, to relieve the troubles of the sick and needy people gathered there. So having suggested to Maṇimēkalai that she should visit Ulaka Aṟavi for that purpose, she happily left on her journey to rejoin her husband in the world of demigods.

Maṇimēkalai then set out to visit Ulaka Aṟavi as Kāya Chaṇḍikai had suggested. On her way, she first worshipped at the Sampāpati temple and bowed before Kantil Pāvai. When she reached the house of refuge, she invited all the hungry and disabled people to come forward. When they had gathered round with high expectations, she told them about Amuta Surabi, and how it had formerly belonged to a great soul called Āputtiraṉ. Then with words of comfort she served them food to their complete satisfaction.

9

Utayakumaraṉ tries again

While the people of the city were basking in the warmth of Maṇimēkalai's affection, her grandmother Chitrāpati became enraged to hear that she had embraced Buddhism and become a wandering beggar, feeding the hungry with the help of her begging bowl.

Chitrāpati roundly condemned Maṇimēkalai's actions, because in her view, as a beautiful girl of the courtesan caste, Maṇimēkalai should live with a wealthy man, extract as much money from him as possible, and then leave him when his money ran out. She could not see anything wrong in such behaviour.

Rather, she felt strongly that Maṇimēkalai was now being really stupid: what could have induced her to become a Buddhist nun just at the time when prince Utayakumaraṉ, the heir to the throne of the Chōḻa king, was pursuing her passionately? To reject the prince's proposal, she argued, was like chasing away the angel of wealth and good fortune when it was knocking at her door.

Chitrāpati meets the prince

Chitrāpati was not in a mood to give up, and still believed that she could change the situation. She decided to meet prince Utayakumaraṉ and to encourage him to pursue his aim of winning Maṇimēkalai. She held the hope that she could extract money from the prince by further inflaming his desire for her grand-daughter.

When Chitrāpati reached the palace and announced her arrival to the guard at the gate, she was ushered in without delay. Utayakumaraṉ looked very disappointed that so far he had been unable to make Maṇimēkalai his own. Indeed, the fact that the girl had renounced worldly life and chosen the life of a recluse had put him off. When Chitrāpati paid him this unexpected visit, he was greatly cheered and welcomed her eagerly. In fact, he jumped to the conclusion that she had come with some good news.

Without more ado, Chitrāpati apologized for the treatment he had received from Sutamati, and promised that she would cooperate with him fully in his attempt to woo Maṇimēkalai. Chitrāpati spoke in such glowing terms that the prince's desire for Maṇimēkalai which had rather cooled of late, now blazed up afresh and his fading hopes took on a new lease of life.

The prince's passion is revived

Overjoyed by Chitrāpati's confidence, the prince told her without reserve of all the pain he had been suffering because Maṇimēkalai had not returned his love. He confided to her that his longing for Maṇimēkalai had filled every tissue of his being, and that he could not live without her.

He went on to say that it was the deadly warning he had received from the deity in front of the Crystal Hall where Maṇimēkalai had taken refuge that had tormented him most. In fact, that warning had more or less succeeded in putting him off pursuing her.

Chitrāpati warned Utayakumaraṉ that there was no point in listening to anyone, either human or divine. She advised him that if he had set his mind on any object, then he must be totally focused on that one aim. She went on to say that nothing comes easily, and that there will always be pain and obstacles to overcome. She reminded him of the old saying: no pain, no gain.

Just as a blacksmith strikes a red hot piece of iron on the anvil with ever greater vigour when he finds it becoming more and more malleable, Chitrāpati began to manipulate the prince ever more forcefully, and he fell an easy prey to her wiles. He reassured himself that all was not lost, as he had at first thought, and that he could still bring Maṇimēkalai round to his own way of thinking.

The prince meets Maṇimēkalai

Now convinced that after all Maṇimēkalai could indeed be won, Utayakumaraṉ set out to find her. After thanking Chitrāpati profusely, he went directly to the Ulaka Ar̲avi where he guessed Maṇimēkalai would be. There he saw her with the wonderful rice bowl in her hand, wearing the dress of a Buddhist nun.

The prince went up to her and hesitatingly asked her why she wanted to renounce the world. This time the prince was polite in his approach, though his face clearly revealed the warmth of his passion for her.

Maṇimēkalai was taken aback by such a direct question from this unexpected visitor. However, she kept in mind what she had recently been told, that this very Utayakumaran̲ had been her husband in her previous birth. This knowledge made her feel very uneasy, and it began to weaken her resolve to renounce all earthly ties.

She was not sure how she should react if he made advances to her or began to behave improperly. On the one hand, she did not want to ignore him if he were to take her hand; on the other, she could not easily forget her decision to become a nun. While these conflicting impulses raged within her, she boldly began to give the prince the benefit of her advice.

Maṇimēkalai evades the prince

"Your highness," she began. "What is your opinion of this body? It can fall sick; it can become disabled; one day all of a sudden it may die, whether by reason of disease or from no known cause. That is its very nature. Since that is so, I decided to do something that would be of practical benefit to the community while I am still young and healthy. The truth is that youth will fade, and our body will not last for ever. So what better course is there for me to take?"

With these words, Maṇimēkalai left the prince abruptly and went inside the Sampāpati temple. Fearing that even there she might be in danger, she chanted the appropriate mantra to disguise herself, and took the form of Kāya Chaṇḍikai, whose disease she had recently cured. So disguised, she left the temple by the main door, while Utayakumaraṉ lay in wait for her outside.

The prince did not understand why Maṇimēkalai had entered the temple in the first place. Now he saw a strange woman leave the temple, but since she bore no resemblance to Maṇimēkalai, he took no notice of her. He was sure that there was no other way by which Maṇimēkalai could leave the temple. So finally, since she did not come out, he grew impatient and went inside to look for her.

Within the temple there were many wonderful statues which looked like real women. Each one of them seemed to be looking directly at him. He examined each one closely to see whether Maṇimēkalai was concealed among them, but he could not find her.

In perplexity, he appealed to all the gods to reveal her whereabouts, and took a vow not to leave the place until he found her. So with renewed determination Utayakumaraṉ went outside and resumed his watch at the entrance, hoping for Maṇimēkalai eventually to show herself.

As the prince waited there in agony, a voice rang out from the sky: "You foolish prince! You have made a vow without thinking through its consequences."

When Utayakumaraṉ heard these words he was deeply shaken, and called to mind the warning which the god had given him earlier at the Crystal Hall. Comparing that warning with the present one, he was left deeply confused. He could not understand why the deity interfered every time he was close to catching up with his beloved Maṇimēkalai.

The prince connected these strange incidents with the divine rice bowl which Maṇimēkalai was carrying in her hand. That thought made him more frightened than confused. So, feeling disinclined to wait there any longer, he quickly left the temple. In the hope of soon finding Maṇimēkalai again, he returned to the palace to draw up a plan.

10

The prison reformed

After leaving the temple disguised as Kāya Chaṇḍikai, Maṇimēkalai made her way to the city prison. There, without the knowledge of the warders, she met each prisoner and enquired about the offences for which they had been sentenced to imprisonment. She spoke to them kindly, with gentle words of comfort and advice. Then she gave them all a hearty meal from her magic bowl, and left the prison having succeeded in bringing about a complete change in their attitude to life.

The inmates became penitent, and their behaviour was reformed beyond recognition. On the following day, the guards observed this dramatic change for the better in the conduct of the prisoners. On further investigation, they learnt that this transformation was the direct result of Maṇimēkalai's visit.

The guards then decided that they should inform the king of the sudden change in the hearts and minds of the prisoners, some of whom had previously been dangerous and hardened criminals. So the chief warder set out to the palace to meet the king, Kiḷḷivaḷavaṉ.

When the king heard the chief warder's report of the strange reformation that had taken place in the prisoners, he was stunned. He could not believe that a woman could do in a single day all that his prison system had been unable to achieve in years. So the king sent his men to fetch Maṇimēkalai immediately.

The king is persuaded

In obedience to the king's command, Maṇimēkalai went to the palace still disguised as Kāya Chaṇḍikai, with Amuta Surabi in her hand. As she approached the king, she greeted him, curtseyed and bowed her head low in obeisance.

"Who are you?" the king asked, "And what is this rice bowl that you are carrying in your hand?"

In reply, Maṇimēkalai told him a white lie. She said that her name was Kāya Chaṇḍikai, that her father was a celestial being, and that she had received the rice bowl from a deity whom she had met at Ulaka Aṟavi. She also described the great service she was performing for the hungry with the help of the rice bowl. She did not omit to mention that she had also cured a lady who had been suffering from an incurable disease.

King Kiḷḷivaḷavaṉ believed all that Maṇimēkalai told him. He was so pleased with her outstanding service to suffering humanity that he praised her in glowing terms and asked if she was expecting any reward from him.

Snatching at this offer, she told the king that because she had reformed its inmates, there was no longer any need for the prison; moreover, all the prisoners should now be set free, and all the prisons in the country should be converted into charitable houses for sages and saints. The king readily agreed to this request and the country was rid of all its prisons. Having achieved this major reform, Maṇimēkalai returned to Ulaka Aṟavi, still in disguise as Kāya Chaṇḍikai.

The beneficial changes which she had brought about greatly pleased the citizens of the country. Many of the prisons were transformed into Buddhist temples, nursing homes and places of refuge. Everybody started talking about the wonderful deeds that Maṇimēkalai had performed. Meanwhile Utayakumaraṉ was still making plans to abduct Maṇimēkalai. Believing her still to be at Ulaka Aṟavi, he hoped to kidnap her as soon as she set foot outside the door. So he went to the house of refuge and waited for her there, unseen by anyone.

11

The death of the prince

Unaware of the fact that the real Kāya Chaṇḍikai had been cured of her illness and that she had returned to her own world, her husband Kāñchaṉaṉ soon came to earth looking for her. He reached Ulaka Aṟavi, and there he saw Maṇimēkalai disguised as Kāya Chaṇḍikai with the rice bowl in her hand. When he saw her, he was very happy to have found his wife, little realizing that it was in fact Maṇimēkalai in disguise whom he had seen.

When Kāñchaṉaṉ began to speak to Maṇimēkalai in loving tones, she did not know who he was. So she remained indifferent to his affectionate words, and went on busily distributing food from her rice bowl to the many hungry people gathered there. Kāñchaṉaṉ could only stand there, watching her with astonishment.

Through the corner of her eye, Maṇimēkalai noticed that Kāñchaṉaṉ was still watching her intently. Realizing that he must have some hidden motive, she pointed to an old woman in the crowd and began to speak to the people:-

"See the hair of this old lady here. When she was young, her hair was black as a crow. Now that she has grown old, that black hair has become white as a stork. When she was young, everyone praised her crescent-shaped forehead. Today it has shrunk and is full of wrinkles. When she was young, she had a shapely nose like the beak of a parrot. Now it has lost its shape, and it is running the whole time. Today she has lost her pearly teeth, and her cheeks are sunken. Her breasts were once admired by all, but now they sag shapelessly."

When Kāñchaṉaṉ heard Maṇimēkalai speak these words, he thought they were directed at him, and drew the conclusion that his own wife had become disenchanted with him. Burning with rage, he could not believe that his wife could have changed so suddenly and lost all interest in him. So he withdrew from the scene, and hid in the bushes nearby to see what would happen next.

Just then, Kāñchaṉaṉ noticed from his hiding place that another man too was watching all that was going on. Maṇimēkalai's words about the old lady made him think that that other man, who was none other than Utayakumaraṉ, must be his wife's secret lover.

Utayakumaraṉ is assassinated

In the meantime, Maṇimēkalai secretly left Ulaka Aṟavi and went to the Sampāpati temple close by, with both Utayakumaraṉ and Kāñchaṉaṉ still watching outside. It was nearly nightfall, but there was still no sign of Maṇimēkalai coming out of the house. Although Utayakumaraṉ became impatient, he was intelligent enough to see through Maṇimēkalai's disguise, and he realized that she had been speaking directly to him.

As a result, the prince concluded that Maṇimēkalai had deliberately taken the form of Kāya Chaṇḍikai in order to deny him his long-awaited opportunity. So he decided to carry her off that very night. Having made his decision, Utayakumaraṉ went off to make the necessary preparations.

Meanwhile Kāñchaṉaṉ was still unaware that Maṇimēkalai had slipped away to the Sampāpati temple. Nevertheless, on the strength of his mistaken belief that his wife had fallen in love with another man, he decided to take the drastic step of murdering that man when next he came to meet her.

Believing that her lover would soon be back, he lay in wait for his return outside Ulaka Aṟavi. With sword in hand and murder in mind, Kāñchaṉaṉ remained concealed close to where he had last seen her.

On the stroke of midnight, Utayakumaraṉ returned to Ulaka Aṟavi, ready to carry off Maṇimēkalai as he had planned. He was stealthily making his way towards the gate of the house of refuge when Kāñchaṉaṉ spotted him. Now confirmed in his belief that this man was indeed his wife's lover, Kāñchaṉaṉ was not minded to wait any longer. So he sprang out from his hiding place and slew Utayakumaraṉ with a single blow.

12

Kantil Pāvai intervenes

With Utayakumaraṉ slain, Kāñchaṉaṉ turned towards the spot where he had last seen Maṇimēkalai a few hours previously. Suddenly there rang out a divine voice from one of the statues on the temple pillar :-

"Kāñchaṉaṉ! You have made a terrible blunder! In your mad rage, you have taken leave of your senses. Your wife Kāya Chaṇḍikai left this town a long time ago. The woman whom you saw was not your wife but Maṇimēkalai, who had taken your wife's form in order to avoid Utayakumaraṉ. The man you slew was none other than Utayakumaraṉ, the prince. He came here to kidnap Maṇimēkalai against her will. Now he has been punished for his wicked plan, and met his end in accordance with his *karma*."

When he heard the words of the statue, Kāñchaṉaṉ was aghast. He trembled as he realized what a dreadful deed he had committed, and in panic he made a hasty escape from the scene of the crime.

While that drama was unfolding outside Ulaka Aṟavi, Maṇimēkalai was sleeping peacefully inside the Sampāpati temple, unaware of the ugly scenes that were being enacted so near at hand. Soon the news of the murder of Utayakumaran̲ spread abroad and reached the temple where Maṇimēkalai was sleeping. At once she awoke, rose to her feet and rushed out. There she saw the body of the dead prince.

Although she had become a nun, Maṇimēkalai could not easily forget that Utayakumaran̲ had been her husband in her previous birth. She now laid aside her disguise and resumed her own form. Weeping uncontrollably, she moved slowly towards the blood-soaked body of the prince. As she did so, the statue of Kantil Pāvai on the temple pillar cried out:

"Do not go near Utayamumaran̲'s body! He might well have been your husband in a previous birth, but since you are striving to break the chain of birth, it is not right for you to mourn for him."

Hearing this, Maṇimēkalai realized that she had made a momentary mistake, and obeyed the command of Kantil Pāvai. She begged the god to reveal to her what had happened to Utayakumaran̲ in his previous birth.

"All powerful god!" she pleaded. "You reveal the past to all who visit this place. Please will you explain this to me: why in his prevous birth was Utayakumaran̲, then known as Rākulan̲, bitten by the snake Tiṭṭi? And why now has the prince come to so violent an end? What is the connection between these two unfortunate events?"

Further revelations about Maṇimēkalai's past

Kantil Pāvai realized Maṇimēkalai's distress, but his words only fired her curiosity the more. "In your previous births," he began, "you and your husband were in the habit of venerating a sage called Brahma Tarumaṉ who lived near the bank of a river called Kāyaṅkarai. With the help of your servant, you and your husband Rākulaṉ were supporting the sage by providing food for him each day.

"One day you asked your servant to come early in the morning to prepare the food. Unfortunately, the servant delayed and came very late. Then in the kitchen he tripped over a cooking vessel and hurt his foot. Instead of pitying the servant, in anger your husband slew him on the spot. This was a grievous sin.

"It was that sin which resulted in Rākulaṉ being bitten by the snake. That sin was also the cause for Utayakumaraṉ's death at the hand of Kāya Chaṇḍikai's husband, Kāñchaṉaṉ."

Maṇimēkalai seemed somewhat comforted by Kantil Pāvai's explanation. However, when the statuette went on to foretell the future for Maṇimēkalai herself, its predictions weighed heavily upon her.

The god then told her that he was a celestial being whose real name was Tuvatikaṉ. Moreover, the statuette on the temple pillar in which he had been residing was to be the place where he would continue to live in the future.

13

The prince's funeral

The murder of Utayakumaraṉ attracted the whole town to Chakkaravāḷa Kōṭṭam early in the morning. When the sages of the place learnt from Maṇimēkalai how Utayakumaraṉ had met his death, they hurried to the palace to report the matter to the king. Having gained audience, they told the king the whole story from beginning to end.

They concluded that the prince was prey to unbridled passion, as was shown in his overwhelming desire for Maṇimēkalai; that Kāñchaṉaṉ held the mistaken belief that Utayakumaraṉ was making advances to his wife Kāya Chaṇḍikai; and it was on the strength of that belief that he had perpetrated the dreadful deed of murdering the king's son and heir.

The sages expected that the king would try to defend his son's actions, however culpable they might have seemed. But even before the sages had finished their tale, the king came to the conclusion that his son deserved the punishment meted out to him by providence. So remaining composed, king Kiḷḷivaḷavaṉ declared:

"Venerable sages! As you will see, there is nothing to feel sorry about in the death of the prince. Of course, Utayakumaraṉ is my dear son and heir. But that does not mean that he is to be judged under a different set of rules from anyone else. Everyone must be held to be equal before the law.

"From what you have said, and I have no reason not to believe you, I am convinced that my son was in the wrong. Rather than me pronouncing the death sentence upon him, the celestial being Kāñchaṉaṉ has punished him instead. I belong to a line of kings famed for the justice of their rule. One killed his own son by running over him in his chariot, when he learnt that the lad had carelessly killed a calf in the same manner. I thank you for bringing me this news. Now you may take your leave."

When the sages had left, full of admiration for the king's decision, the king commanded that Maṇimēkalai be arrested and detained at once. Then he summoned his ministers and ordered them to arrange for the prince's funeral.

The king wanted his son to be cremated before word reached the kings of the neighbouring countries that his son had met his death as the result of his own wicked actions. So the funeral of the prince took place in a low key, although the people of the palace, including the king himself, still mourned the death in private.

The king felt that the manner in which his son came to his death was not worthy of being marked by a public funeral. Accordingly, he issued orders to the gatekeepers that he did not wish to receive the customary condolences. So the people who gathered in large numbers to offer him their sympathy were politely turned away at the gate. And, as ordered by the king, Maṇimēkalai was arrested and detained for investigation in relation to the assassination of the prince.

14

The queen seeks revenge

Now the king had properly aknowledged that it had not been right for Kāñchaṉaṉ to take the law into his own hands. Nevertheless the queen was unhappy that he had publicly declared their son to be in the wrong and therefore deserving of death.

However, although she could not defy the king or alter his judgement, the queen had a different way of thinking about these events. For her, it was because of Maṇimēkalai that her son suffered such an untimely and tragic fate. Now she wanted to avenge his death. Planning to carry out her evil desire by means of a subterfuge, she approached the king and talked to him as if she was fully supporting his judgement.

"Although the dead man is our own son," she said, "we must admit that what he attempted to do was inexcusable. Drunk with a sense of power based on his royal birth, he had tried to kidnap a girl who was simply using her divine bowl to relieve the hunger of the people. In my view, Maṇimēkalai appears to be innocent and does not therefore deserve to be imprisoned."

After speaking these cunning and deceitful words, the queen watched the king for his reaction. His face seemed to beam with happiness. He embraced his wife and said that he was really proud of her for the wise words that she had spoken. He went on to say that he would defer to her wishes and free Maṇimēkalai at once.

The queen thanked the king and expressed her desire to meet Maṇimēkalai as soon as she had been released. The king accordingly ordered the head jailer to set Maṇimēkalai free and to take her to the queen's chambers.

So Maṇimēkalai was led straight away to meet the queen, who greeted her warmly, pretending to love her dearly. In her innocence, Maṇimēkalai failed to realize that the queen was consumed by a burning desire for revenge.

The queen then surreptitiously gave Maṇimēkalai a poisoned drink in order to take away her power of reason. However, because Maṇimēkalai was blessed with magical powers, the poisonous concoction failed to have any effect on her.

Having failed in her first attempt, the queen next tried to bring disgrace on Maṇimēkalai by hiring a villain to enter her room to molest her. When the villain entered Maṇimēkalai's room, she was nowhere to be seen. Instead, by virtue of her magic powers, the villain saw only another sturdy man lying there in her bed. In this way, Maṇimēkalai thwarted all the queen's evil designs.

When the queen found out that all her schemes had been brought to nought, it dawned on her that Maṇimēkalai must be an extraordinary person with supernatural powers.

This realization made the queen fear for her life. She was frightened that, gifted as she was with divine power, Maṇimēkalai might cause her harm. So she hurried to the room where Maṇimēkalai was, fell down before her and begged to be forgiven for all the evil that she had planned against her.

Maṇimēkalai reveals the prince's past

Maṇimēkalai replied that she did not deserve to be treated with such respect by the queen of the country; rather it was the queen who deserved to be venerated by her.

"For one thing," Maṇimēkalai reasoned, "you are the queen of this country. Moreover, you are the mother of Utayakumaraṉ who was my husband in my previous birth, when he bore the name Rākulaṉ. As such, you could be called my mother-in-law. So it is you who deserve respect and honour from me. It was for these reasons that I bore with courage all the attacks that you launched against me."

The queen listened with rapt attention while Maṇimēkalai told her the details of Utayakumaraṉ's previous birth. When Maṇimēkalai had finished her story, all the queen's rage against her melted away, and she became quiet and reasonable. She thanked Maṇimēkalai with a sense of shame and penitence, and invited her to stay with her at the palace for a couple of days.

Maṇimēkalai thanked the queen for her kind invitation, which she would very much like to have accepted. However, she would spend only one night with her in the palace, since she still had a lot of work to do for the needy.

Chitrāpati tries again

When the sad news of Utayakumaraṉ's death reached the ears of Chitrāpati, she felt that all her dreams had been shattered. However, the news that Maṇimēkalai had been imprisoned following the prince's death then became her chief anxiety.

She thought that she could do something to help Maṇimēkalai by pleading with the queen. She also hoped that after obtaining her realease, she could persuade Maṇimēkalai to reverse her decision to become a nun. Accordingly, she gained permission at the palace to have an audience with the queen.

Chitrāpati was unaware that Maṇimēkalai had already been released from the prison, and that the queen had already been put fully in the picture. So in the queen's presence, Chitrāpati began talking in a round about manner. After listening to Chitrāpati for a while, the queen cut her short. She told her bluntly that Maṇimēkalai would not have any dealings with people of dubious character, and that she herself would always be on Maṇimēkalai's side.

Shocked by this unexpected turn, Chitrāpati was furious and had no idea what to do next. Throughout the meeting, Maṇimēkalai was in the adjoining room listening to all that was said.

15

Maṇimēkalai begins her life work

Unaware of all that had happened in the palace after the death of Utayakumaraṉ and the arrest of Maṇimēkalai, Mātavi and Sutamati hurried to Aṟavaṇa Aḍikaḷ to seek his advice. The sage agreed to meet the king and the queen on their behalf, and went off with them to the palace. When the three of them arrived at the palace, Chitrāpati was still there, perplexed and angry.

As soon as the queen saw Aṟavaṇa Aḍikaḷ, she rose up and greeted him. She sat him down on a chair and declared that she was honoured and blessed by his coming. Maṇimēkalai then came into the chamber, bowed low and paid homage to the sage. As was his wont, Aṟavaṇa Aḍikaḷ spoke a few words of wise advice, to which they all listened with attention.

When they saw Maṇimēkalai standing there looking none the worse for all her adventures, the anxieties that had been weighing so heavily on Mātavi and Sutamati all dissolved, and they breathed a sigh of relief. Aṟavaṇa Aḍikaḷ too felt that the problem he had come to address had already been resolved. So he looked at Maṇimēkalai and said:

"My dear Maṇimēkalai, now that you know all about your past, you must begin to think of your future. This is my command to you: your task is to study the teachings of all other living faiths in this country. When you have done that, you may come and see me again, and I will teach you more about the philosophy of Buddhism."

With these words, Aṟavaṇa Aḍikaḷ stood up to leave, and bade them all good bye. But Maṇimēkalai came before him and fell at his feet. She then addressed all those present with her in the room.

"My dear friends!" she declared. "You are all to follow whatever advice and teaching the venerable Aṟavaṇa Aḍikaḷ may give you. But as for me, if I remain in this city, those who do not know the truth abouth the death of the prince will continue to blame me for it.

"So I now plan to visit the country where Āputtiraṉ lives in his present birth. Then I will go to the great city of Vañchi, to worship the statue of Kaṇṇaki at her shrine. After that I shall devote myself to my charitable work in earnest. None of you need feel any anxiety on my account."

Maṇimēkalai leaves for Nāvalam

After bidding a fond farewell to all her friends gathered there, Maṇimēkalai left the palace and travelled invisibly through the sky to the island of Nāvalam, which was ruled by a king called Puṇṇiyarāsaṉ. Upon arriving there, she sought out a flower garden near the capital of that country.

There she called on a renowned Buddhist teacher called Taruma Chāvakan̲ and paid him homage.

At that time the monk had with him a couple of distinguished visitors. Nevertheless, he welcomed Maṇimēkalai and offered her a chair. As soon as she was seated, the monk addressed one of his visitors, who was no less a person than king Puṇṇiyarāsan̲. The monk asked the king whether he knew who the young lady was with the divine begging bowl. The king had no idea; so the monk paused for a minute, then to relieve the king's embarrassment, he said:

"In the whole of this island of Nāvalam, there is no one as famous as this great lady. Some time ago when we went to Pūmpukār to make the acquaintance of king Kiḷḷivaḷavan̲, I remember telling you that Ar̲avaṇa Aḍikaḷ had spoken very highly of her".

When the monk had finished his introduction, Maṇimēkalai spoke to king Puṇṇiyarāsan̲ with a pleasant smile.

"Have you forgotten this bowl which is now in my possession?" she asked. "This is the very same Amuta Surabi which you held in your hand in a previous birth. You may not remember that, but you could at least have recalled that in this birth you were born in the womb of a cow! If you were to visit the island of Maṇipallavam and there worshipped at the seat of the Buddha, you will certainly learn more about your previous birth. So that is a place you should definitely visit."

With this suggestion, Maṇimēkalai again became invisible, and flew away towards

Maṇipallavam, leaving the king in a state of bewilderment. After she had left, the king of Nāvalam, who had been Āputtiraṉ in his previous birth, began to think about that former life of his.

Everything gradually began to become clear to him, and a faint memory of every single incident began to return. He recalled that in his present birth he had been born from the womb of a cow, that he had been brought up by a sage called Maṇmukaṉ, and that a childless king called Būmi Chandran had adopted him.

Maṇimēkalai at Maṇipallavam

Maṇimēkalai was very hopeful that Puṇṇiyarāsaṉ would not fail to visit Maṇipallavam, and she was expecting him every day. When finally he arrived, Maṇimēkalai was extremely happy. First she took him for a walk round the island, then she led him to the Buddha's Holy Seat. When he made obeisance before it, he began to remember more clearly all the incidents in his previous birth. Overwhelmed with joy and excitement, he said:

"Oh god of Maṇipallavam! To whom could I confess the pain and sorrow that I suffered that night when I was unable to feed the crowd of people who had come to me begging for food? It was when I was waiting there helpless that Sintātēvi appeared to me and presented me with the magic bowl. She told me that with that bountiful bowl I could feed any number of people.

From that time on, I could never forget the feet of god."

Puṇṇiyarāsaṉ was filled with joy and felt greatly relieved. After walking round the island together a couple of times more, they made their way towards the Kōmuki tank, where they sat down under the laurel trees and relaxed.

As they were sitting there, unaware of what was happening around them, Tīvatilakai, the guardian deity of the island, approached. The king quickly rose to his feet and fell down before her. The goddess then told him all the further details of his previous birth, at which he was struck with awe and amazement.

Maṇimēkalai was delighted to have been able to help the king acquire all this information, and urged him now to return to his country to continue serving his people, She then bade him good bye and left for the Chēra country.

As she was flying through the sky, she saw below her the memorial shrine that had been set up for Kaṇṇaki and Kōvalaṉ in the city of Vañchi. She descended to the earth at that spot, and solemnly paid her homage before the shrine.

Maṇimēkalai spent a couple of days there, and then began her work in earnest, alleviating the sufferings of human kind and spreading the message of the Buddha, who was born to free all humanity from ignorance, sin and poverty.

EPILOGUE

At the time when the action of the twin epics took place, there were three Tamil kingdoms in South India, as noted in the Introduction. They were each ruled by kings who inherited the throne from their fathers and expected to pass it on to their eldest sons when they died. They had absolute power of life and death over their subjects, but they were expected strictly to uphold justice and fairness for all in the way that they used their power.

The three Tamil kingdoms were not always friendly to one another. Sometimes they made alliances, at other times they fought wars with their neighbours. The last part of the Silappatikāram tells of the war waged by the Chēra king against an alliance of non-Tamil kings who ruled in northern India. In addition, there appear to have been Roman and Greek settlements in the Tamil-speaking region at this period.

It is clear from the story of the epics that the Tamil people of that time enjoyed a highly sophisticated culture. According to ancient tradition, three learned academies based in the city of Maturai had one after the other nurtured and developed that culture. Of the two earliest academies, known by their Tamil name as

Sangams, we have no reliable information. From the period of the third Sangam, however, which covers roughly the first three centuries of the Christian era, and possibly the last two centuries before that, a good deal of literature has survived.

The literature of this third Sangam period consists almost entirely of individual poems, containing anything from three lines to several hundred lines. These poems deal mainly with matters of love and of war. There also survives, perhaps from the pre-Christian era, a comprehensive text book of grammar, the Tolkāppiyam. This work deals not only with the details of grammar and poetic metre, but also lays down the rules which govern how the poets are to handle the topics of love and war in their poems, and the rules of good social and personal conduct.

The characters who play a part in the Silappatikāram are usually described as engaged in some particular work or profession. For example, they may be merchants or cowherds or priests or musicians. However, it does not seem that the caste system which we know in India today was rigidly in place at that time in the Tamil regions, with one exception. Brahmins are mentioned as already having a position of special honour among the people, not only for their religious duties, but also as advisers to the king.

What do we know then about the author of the Silappatikāram, and how it came to be written? Tradition names its author as Iḷaṅkō Aḍikaḷ. He was a prince of the Chēra line, and the younger son of king Imayavarampaṉ Neḍuñchēralātaṉ. Some scholars reject that tradition, and think that the author was an unknown poet who collected the stories of Kōvalaṉ and Kaṇṇaki which had long been current as folk tales among the Tamils and gave them their present written form.

There is, however, a story about Iḷaṅkō which finds a place in the poem itself. This tells how one day an astrologer came to the court of his father, and predicted that Iḷaṅkō would be the next king rather than his elder brother, who would by rights have expected to inherit the throne. Not wishing to embarrass his brother, Iḷaṅkō immediately left the palace. He renounced the world and became a Jain monk.

This story, if we can accept it as reliable, gives us a clue as to when the Silappātikaram was written. For it gives the name of Iḷaṅkō's elder brother as Cheṅkuṭṭuvaṉ, who is known from other sources to have reigned as Chēra king in the second century CE. This is the Cheṅkuṭṭuvaṉ who plays a major role in the third part of the Silappatikāram.

This fits also with the mention of king Gajabāhu of Lanka, who we are told attended the ceremony for the dedication of the temple of Kaṇṇaki at Vañchi. He is known to have come to the throne in the year 171 CE. On this reckoning, the Silappatikāram is likely to have been written late in the second century CE, towards the end of the period of the third Sangam, not long after the events happened of which it tells.

If Iḷaṅkō Aḍikaḷ, a Jain monk, was the author of this poem, that also explains another of its characteristics. As mentioned earlier, we know that there were many Jains among the Tamil people at that time. Iḷaṅkō Aḍikaḷ's poem makes frequent mention of that religion, and in particular gives an especially favourable picture of the Jain nun, Kavunti Aḍikaḷ, who acted as Kōvalaṉ's spiritual guide on his journey to Maturai in the second part of the epic.

Whoever was the author of the Silappatikāram, whether it was indeed Iḷaṅkō Aḍikaḷ or someone else, we can be sure from reading the poem that he was a highly skilled and learned poet. He composed his poem in a classical Tamil poetic metre. He also enriched his work by including a large number of short poems written in the traditional forms of Tamil poetry.

In one important respect, Iḷaṅkō's work broke new ground in the field of Tamil literature. Before his time, in Sanskrit there had already been composed epics of enormous length, the Rāmāyana and the Mahābhārata. But nothing like them had been written in Tamil, so far as we know. The Silappatikāram is not as long as the two classical Sanskrit epics, but it is a long, unified poem that tells a continuous story. And following Iḷaṅkō's lead, there soon came to be written other epic poems in Tamil, such as the Maṇimēkalai and the Chīvakacintāmaṇi.

Although he was brought up as a royal prince, and later in life became a Jain monk, in his poem Iḷaṅkō shows an amazing breadth of knowledge and experience. He was familiar with the intricate technicalities of Tamil music and dance. He could write convincingly about the lives of people from widely different backgrounds, from courtesans to religious ascetics, and from kings to cowherds. He gives us full and vivid descriptions of natural scenery and of social customs. He was bold enough to make an ordinary woman the central figure in his story, and to tell how she challenged and put to shame the male-dominated power structure of the time. In short, using his own experience, his powers of observation and imagination, and his great poetic gifts, Iḷaṅkō has given us a detailed and colourful picture of the lives of the Tamil people of his age.

For this reason, the Silappatikāram has always remained popular among Tamil readers. However, it takes a considerable familiarity with classical Tamil for anyone today to read and appreciate the epic in its original form. That is why in the last two centuries, many different versions of the story of Kōvalaṉ and Kaṇṇaki have been produced, in Tamil and English, in prose and verse, in musical and dramatic forms.

When the reader first comes to the Maṇimēkalai in this book after reading the Silappātikaram, and turns the first pages, s/he will at once recognize some of the main characters as familiar.

It is a striking fact that in both these epics women are the main actors, and show a strength of character and purpose which far surpasses that of the male participants in the two stories. In the Silappatikāram, it is Kaṇṇaki who stands out by her loyalty and courage, for which she is finally rewarded by being acknowledged as a goddess. In the Maṇimēkalai, the heroine, though not immune from doubt and conflict, eventually holds fast to her resolve to renounce the world by becoming a Buddhist nun, while the important men around her are slaves of passion and delusion.

Tamil literary tradition ties the two epics even more closely together, by assigning the authorship of the Maṇimēkalai to the poet Sāttaṉār. This figure appears in the closing scene of the Silappatikāram at the dedication of the statue of Kaṇṇaki, and was reputedly a colleague or contemparary of Iḷaṅkō Aḍikaḷ, the Silappatikāram's author. He is said to have been a dealer in grain, and to have been a scholar noted for his grammatical fastidiousness.

If that tradition is accepted as reliable, then the two epics will have been composed at more or less the same period. As we saw above, the historical dating of the Chēra monarch Cheṅkuṭṭuvaṉ and king Gajabāhu of Lanka towards the end of the second century CE, would fix the composition of the Silappatikāram in that period. That means that the Maṇimēkalai too will have been written at about the same time, towards the end of the Sangam period in the history of Tamil literature. By reason of these manifold connections, the Silappatikāram and the Maṇimēkalai are commonly referred to as the "twin epics" (iraṭṭaik kāppiyaṅkaḷ).

In spite of this close relationship, there are also significant differences between the two poems. The most obvious one concerns their religious atmosphere and background. In the Silappatikāram, the Jain religion is favourably represented in the person of the elderly nun, Kavunti Aḍikaḷ, who is the sympathetic guide and mentor of Kaṇṇaki and Kōvalaṉ on their journey to Maturai. But, besides a number of Hindu deities such as Koṟṟavai and Murukaṉ, Buddhism too receives a favourable mention in the part played by the Buddhist monk, Aṟavaṇa Aḍikaḷ. So the overall atmosphere in this epic is tolerant and inclusive.

In the Maṇimēkalai, however, the religious atmosphere is markedly different. The whole story is based on the journey of the heroine towards her goal of becoming a Buddhist nun, in which again Aṟavaṇa Aḍikaḷ plays a major part. However, in contrast to the author of the Silappatikāram, this poet is not averse to portraying other religions in an unfavourable light. For example, in the story of Sutamati's experience, the Jain monks refused to give any practical assistance to her father in his hour of need, whereas at the Buddhist monastery by contrast he was given a welcome and timely aid.

In this way, the author of the Maṇimēkalai seems to be engaged in an attempt to propagate one particular religion, namely Buddhism, at the expense of other religions which were practised among the Tamil people of his time. This purpose is also reflected in the long passages in this epic that are devoted to the elucidation of Buddhist teaching and philosophy. As a result, the author has had to use many words of Pali and Sanskrit origin, to the extent that more than ten percent of the vocabulary of the Maṇimēkalai consists of non-Tamil words imported from those languages.

This difference in religious orientation between the two epics contributes to a further difference between them. Whereas in the Silappatikāram, the narrative is interspersed with poems and songs perhaps drawn from folk or traditional sources, the Maṇimēkalai includes no such elements. Instead, the narrative here is interspersed with lengthy religious and philosophical discourses that commend the Buddhist faith.

Here and there throughout the narrative of the Maṇimēkalai, we also find included the background stories of major characters such as Sutamati, Āputtiraṉ and Kāya Chaṇḍikai. These form interludes in the progression of the story, like flashbacks in a modern film. So in addition to the difference in religious outlook, we find a noticeable structural difference as well.

What are we to say then in conclusion about the origin of the Maṇimēkalai? Many conservative Tamil scholars would hold to the traditional view that it belongs to the late second century CE. They would accept the authorship of Sāttaṉār and the close connection with the Silappatikāram as described above.

Other scholars, however, would place it later in the development of Tamil literature, perhaps in the fifth century CE. Among the reasons for this view are the fact that it was not until the period between the fourth and sixth centuries CE that the

Jain and Buddhist religions assumed a place of dominance among the Tamil people, such as we see in both these epics. Indeed, the Periya Purāṇam depicts a period of inter-religious conflict among the Tamils, probably in the sixth and seventh centuries, similar to what is reflected in the Maṇimēkalai.

However, all that having been said, the date of composition is not the most important thing about this epic. What grips the reader is the way that character is portrayed and the story unfolds. The figure of Maṇimēkalai herself captures our interest, so that we become concerned about the outcome of her adventures. Across the ages, she comes over as a recognisably human person, with hopes and fears, doubts and conflicts. In addition, this epic gives us a graphic picture of Tamil society in a byegone age, particularly in respect of the religious context of the time, and also in respect of the relationship between the sexes.

Appendix A

Guide to the transliteration of Tamil letters

The system followed here is basically that prescribed by the University of Madras Tamil Lexicon. However, a strict following of those rules would in some cases give the English reader a seriously misleading idea of how a letter is to be pronounced. Therefore in this book exceptions to the rules have been made in the case of a few consonants. It is hoped that this revised usage will more accurately represent the way the letters concerned are actually pronounced.

Vowels:

அ	- a	ஆ	- ā
இ	- i	ஈ	- ī
உ	- u	ஊ	- ū
எ	- e	ஏ	- ē
ஐ	- ai	ஒ	- o
ஓ	- ō	ஔ	- au
ஃ	- k̲		

Consonants:

க்	- k	ங்	- ṅ
ச்	- s, ch	ஞ்	- ñ
ட்	- ṭ , ḍ	ண்	- ṇ
த்	- t	ந்	- n
ப்	- p,b	ம்	- m
ய்	- y	ர்	- r
ல்	- l	வ்	- v
ழ்	- l̲	ள்	- ḷ
ற்	- r̲	ன்	- n̲

Notes:

1) The Tamil retroflex ட் should according to the rules strictly always be ṭ; but after the retroflex nasal ண், and in the middle of a word between two vowels, this letter is transliterated as ḍ; when the letter is doubled, ṭṭ is used.

2) The Tamil bilabial ப் should always be p; but between two vowels in the middle of a word, this letter is transliterated here as b.

3) The Tamil letter ச் should always be c; but in the middle of a word between two vowels, s is used; when doubled and after the nasal ஞ், ch is used; at the beginning of a word, either s or ch is used, according to whichever is closer to current Tamil pronunciation.

4) The forms of some names of Sanskrit origin which are current in English are preserved in their familiar spellings, rather than strictly transliterated from their Tamil form (e.g. *Lakshmi, Buddha*, etc.)

Appendix B

Guide to the pronunciation of Tamil words

These rough notes on the pronunciation of Tamil names are included for readers who do not speak Tamil, and for Tamil speakers who are not familiar with the system which is followed in ths book.

1) Vowels: each vowel is pronounced in the same way wherever it occurs (unlike English):

a - as u in "cut"	[e.g. *Kaṇṇaki*]
ā - as a in "can't"	[*Ātirai*]
i - as i in "kit"	[*Chitrāpati*]
ī - as ee in "keep"	[*Vīrai*]
u - as u in "put"	[*Sutamati*]
ū - as oo in "coot"	[*Pūmpukār*]
e - as e in "kept"	[*Cheṅkuṭṭuvaṉ*]
ē - as a in "care"	[*Chēra*]
ai - as i in "kite"	[*Ayyai*]
o – as o in "cot"	[*Potikai*]
ō – as oa in "coal"	[*Chōḻa*]
au - as ou in "pout"	[*Kausikaṉ*]

2) As for Tamil retroflex consonants (ṭ/ḍ, ṇ, ḷ and ḻ): there are no direct English equivalents. Probably the best that an English speaker can do is to pronounce them like the nearest English

equivalent, i.e. pronounce ṭ as an English t, ḍ as d, ṇ as n, ḷ and ḻ as l [e.g. *Paṭṭiṉam, Aḍikaḷ, Chaṇḍikai, Maṇimēkalai, Chōḻa, Kiḷḷivaḷavaṉ* ,etc.]

3) Other Tamil n's: ṅ usually occurs before k, and the resultant combination ṅk is pronounced like the ng in "anger"; ñ usually occurs before ch, and the resultant ñch is pronounced like nj, as in "banjo". There is virtually no distinction between n and ṉ, which are both pronounced like the ordinary English n. [e.g. *Cheṅkuṭṭuvaṉ, Sañchayaṉ, Kantil, Nīlaṉ*]

4) Tamil r's: in common usage, the two Tamil r's, r and ṟ, are virtually indistinguishable; they are both rolled as in Scots. However, when ṟ is doubled, ṟṟ is pronounced as tr (as in "Patrick"); and where ṟ *follows* ṉ, ṉṟ is pronounced as ndr (as in "Andrew"). [e.g. *Nūṟṟuvar Kaṉṉar, Tiruchenkuṉṟu*]

5) The letters s and ch, used to transliterate the Tamil ச : when s occurs singly between two vowels or at the beginning of a word, it resembles the English s; when ch occurs at the beginning of a word, it is pronounced as ch (as in "chalk"); in the middle of a word, ch is pronounced tch (as in "ketchup"); after ñ, ch is pronounced like the English j (cf. paragraph 4 above). [e.g.*Kausikaṉ, Sāttaṉ, Chēraṉ, Tiruchenkuṉṟu, Kāñchaṉaṉ*]

6) Certain consonants are pronounced differently when used at the beginning of a word from the way they are pronounced when occurring singly in

the middle of a word between two vowels, or after a nasal consonant: e.g. between vowels, k is pronounced as h (as in "ahoy"); between vowels and after n, t is pronounced th (as in "other", "anthem") [e.g. *Maṇimēkalai*, *Mātavi, Kavunti,*]

Appendix C

Key to places and people

(i) Places:

Aṅka Nāḍu	: name of a country
Chakkaravāḷak kōṭṭam	: a sacred area used as a burial ground
Chāvakam	: the ancient name of Sumatra
Chēra country	: the country ruled by the Chēra dynasty
Chōḻa country	: the country ruled by the Chōḻa dynasty
Crystal Hall	: a hall made of crystal in the Uvavaṉam gardens
Ganges, river	: a major river of North India, held to be sacred by the Hindus
Holy Seat	: English translation of *Taruma Āsaṉam* (q.v.)
Kāñchipuram	: a city of South India
Kaṉṉiyākumari	: southernmost point of India
Kāviri, river	: the longest river in the Tamil country, which flows through the Chōḻa kingdom

Kāvirippūm Paṭṭiṉam	: former capital of the Chōḻa kingdom, situated at the mouth of the Kāviri river
Kāyaṅkarai	: a river in India
Kōmuki	: a sacred tank or reservoir for storing water
Koṟkai	: former capital of the Pāṇḍiya Kingdom
Lotus altar	: an altar in the shape of a lotus flower
Lotus feet rock	: a rock bearing the footprints of the Lord Buddha, also known as Pātapaṅkayamalai
Maṇipallavam	: an island lying to the south of India
Maturai	: capital of the Pāṇḍiya kingdom
Nāvalam	: an island in the East Indies
Nilgiri hills	: a range of hills in the Chēra country
Pāṇḍiya country	: the country ruled by the Pāṇḍiya dynasty
Potikai, Mount	: a mountain in the Pāṇḍiya country, near the southern tip of India
Pūmpukār	: another name for Kāvirippūm Paṭṭiṉam
Ratna Tīvu	: island of gem stones
Samanta kūḍam	: a hill in Sri Lanka also known as Samanolimalai

Suḍukāṭṭuk kōṭṭam	: another name for Chakkaravāḷak Kōṭṭam
Taruma Āsaṉam	: a holy seat where the Buddha delivered his teaching
Tavalamalai	: the ancient name for a mountain in Sumatra
Tiruchenkuṉṟu	: a mountain in the Chēra country
Ulaka Aṟavi	: a house of refuge
Uvavaṉam	: a flower garden
Vaikai, river	: the river on which Maturai stands
Vañchi	: the capital of the Chēra kingdom
Vāranāsi	: another name for the Indian city of Kāsi,or Benares

(ii) People :

Akattiyar	: a sage
Amutapati	: wife of Ravivaṉmaṉ
Apañchikaṉ	: husband of Sāli
Āputtiraṉ	: son of Sāli, adopted by Iḷam Pūti
Aṟavaṇa Aḍikaḷ	: a Jain monk
Asalaṉ	: a sage, born from the womb of a cow
Ātirai	: the wife of Chātuvaṉ, who first put food in the begging bowl called Amuta Surabi

Ayyai	: daughter of Mātari, the herdswoman
Bālakumāraṉ	: a Northern king, father of Kaṉakaṉ and Vijayaṉ
Brahma Tarumaṉ	: a Buddhist sage
Būmi Chandraṉ	: the adoptive father of king Puṇṇiyarāsaṉ
Chātuvaṉ	: husband of Ātirai
Cheṅkuṭṭuvaṉ	: a king of the Chēra dynasty
Chēraṉ	: family name of the Chēra kings
Chitrāpati	: a courtesan of Pūmpukār, mother of Mātavi
Chōḻaṉ	: family name of the Chōḻa kings
Damayanti	: wife of king Nala
Durkkai	: goddess of victory, a form of the goddess Pārvati
Eṭṭikumaraṉ	: friend of Utayakumaraṉ
Gajabāhu	: king of ancient Sri Lanka
Iḷam Pūti	: full name of Pūti
Iḷaṅkō Aḍikaḷ	: a prince of the Chēra line, younger brother of Cheṅkuṭṭuvaṉ, author of the Silappatikāram
Imayavarampaṉ Neḍuñchēralātaṉ	Cheṅkuṭṭuvaṉ : a Chēra king, father of
Indra	: ruler of the gods
Kāmaṉ	: the god of love

Kaṉakaṉ : a king of Northern India, son of Bālakumāraṉ

Kāñchaṉaṉ : a celestial being, husband of Kāya Chaṇḍikai

Kaṇṇaki : daughter of Māṉāykaṉ, wife of Kōvalaṉ

Kaṇṇaṉ : Tamil name for Krishna

Kausikaṉ : a Brahmin, friend of Mātavi

Kavunti Aḍikaḷ : a Jain nun, companion of Kōvalaṉ and Kaṇṇaki

Kāya Chaṇḍikai : a celestial being, wife of Kāñchanaṉ

Kēsakampaḷaṉ : a sage born from the womb of a fox

Kiḷḷivaḷavaṉ : a Chōḻa king

Koṟṟavai : the goddess of victory

Kōvalaṉ : merchant of Pūmpukār, son of Māsāttuvāṉ, husband of Kaṇṇaki

Kūṉi : maid of Chitrāpati

Lakshmi : Maṇimēkalai's name in her previous birth

Māḍalaṉ : a Brahmin, known to Kōvalaṉ

Māsāttuvāṉ : merchant of Pūmpukār, father of Kōvalaṉ

Māṉāykaṉ : father of Kaṇṇaki

Maṇimēkalai : daughter of Mātavi and Kōvalaṉ

Maṇimēkalā Teyvam : a female deity

Maṇmukaṉ	: a sage of Tavalamalai, who reared the cow that gave birth to Puṇṇiyarāsaṉ
Maṉu Nīti Chōḻaṉ	: a Chōḻa king renowned for his just rule
Mārutavēkaṉ	: a celestial being who molested Sutamati
Mātari	: a herdswoman, of the Pāṇḍiya country
Mātavi	: a courtesan, daughter of Chitrāpati, and mistress of Kōvalaṉ
Mayaṉ	: celestial architect
Mēṉakai	: a celestial dancer
Murukaṉ	: a god, son of Siva
Nāgas	: ancient inhabitants of Lanka and an adjoining island
Nala	: a king renowned for his justice
Neḍuñcheḻiyaṉ	: a Pāṇḍiya king, responsible for the death of Kōvalaṉ
Nīlaṉ	: general of Cheṅkuṭṭuvaṉ's army
Nūṟṟuvar Kaṉṉar	: a king of Northern India, ally of Cheṅkuṭṭuvaṉ
Pāsāṇṭa Sāttaṉ	: a minor god, cf. Sāttaṉ
Pāṇḍiyaṉ	: family name of the Pāṇḍiya kings
Pattiṉi Tēvi	: the name under which Kaṇṇaki was worshipped as goddess of faithfulness

Piḍāri	: another name for the goddess Kāḷi
Puṇṇiyarāsaṉ	: king of Nāvalam
Pūti	: adoptive father of Āputtiraṉ
Rākuḷaṉ	: name of Utayakumaraṉ in his previous birth, and husband of Maṇimēkalai in her previous birth
Rama	: a mythical king, hero of the Ramayana
Ravivaṉmaṉ	: husband of Amutapati, father of Lakshmi, Tārai and Vīrai
Sādhu Chakkaraṉ	: a sage by whom Maṇimēkalai was blessed in her previous birth
Sampāpati	: guardian deity of Kāvirippūm Paṭṭiṉam
Sañchayaṉ	: ambassador of Nūṟṟuvar Kaṉṉar
Sāttaṉ	: a minor god
Sāttaṉār	: a Tamil poet
Sibi	: a mythical king, renowned for his compassion
Sintātēvi	: giver of Amuta Surabi
Siruṅki	: a sage born in the womb of a deer
Sita	: wife of Rama

Sutamati	: friend of Mātavi, and companion of Maṇimēkalai
Tārai	: Matavi's name in her previous birth
Tārukaṉ	: a demon killed by the goddess Kāḷi
Tēvanti	: companion of Kaṇṇaki
Tilōttamai	: a celestial dancer
Tīvatilakai	: a female deity, guardian of the Buddha's seat on Maṇipallavam
Tuchayaṉ	: king of Kachayam and husband of Tārai & Virai
Tuvatikaṉ	: name of the deity residing in the statue, Kantil Pāvai
Utayakumaraṉ	: a prince of the Chōḻa royal house, son of king Kiḷḷivaḷavaṉ
Vasantamālai	: companion of Mātavi
Vasittar	: a sage
Vēṇmāḷ	: Chēra queen, wife of Cheṅkuṭṭuvaṉ
Veṟṟivēl Cheḻiyaṉ	: Pāṇḍiya king, who succeeded Neḍuñcheḻiyaṉ
Vīrai	: Sutamati's name in her previous birth
Viruchikaṉ	: a sage who cast a spell on Kāya Chaṇḍikai
Viruṅki	: a sage

Vijaya<u>n</u>	: a king of Northern India, son of Bālakumāra<u>n</u>
Villava<u>n</u> Kōtai	: minister of Chēra<u>n</u> Cheṅkuṭṭuva<u>n</u>
Yama<u>n</u>	: the god of death

Appendix D

Glossary of Tamil and Sanskrit words

Aḍikaḷ	: a title given to religious teachers
Akil wood	: a kind of fragrant wood
Amuta Surabi	: a magic rice bowl
Chittirai	: the Tamil month April/May
Indra festival	: an ancient festival held in honour of Indra
Jambo fruit	: rose apple
Kāḷavēkam	: the name of the royal elephant of the Chōḻa king
Kantil Pāvai	: statue of a deity carved on a column in the Sampāpati temple
karma	: action, or fate; the belief that one's actions in one life determine one's fate in the next
kuṅkumam	: saffron; a red pigment worn by Hindu women on their forehead
kuravaik kūttu	: a Tamil country dance
mātavi	: a flowering creeper
mirutaṅkam	: a drum used in South Indian music

prasāḍam	: food offered to a god that is shared with his worshippers
sandal wood	: fragrant wood
sannyāsi	: a recluse or religious mendicant, who has renounced the world
talaikkōl	: a medal presented by kings in former times to outstanding artists
Tiṭṭi	: a deadly poisonous snake
Vaikāsi	: the Tamil month of May/June
vēṅkai	: a yellow flowering tree
yāḻ	: a South Indian stringed musical instrument
yōgi	: an ascetic who practises strict mental discipline

About the Authors

Sellathamby Sriskandarajah was born in Sri Lanka. After graduating from the University of Madras, he became an Advocate of the Supreme Court of Sri Lanka, and worked in the Ministry of Justice as Crown Counsel and then as Senior Legal Draftsman until 1980. Subsequently he moved to Nigeria, where he taught English and Law. After coming to England, he joined the Government Legal Service and served as a Principal Legal Officer until his retirement. Mr Sriskandarajah has written many books and articles on law and Tamil literature, both in English and Tamil.

Robin McGlashan studied classics at Oxford and theology at Cambridge, and then taught for ten years at the Tamil Nadu Theological Seminary at Maturai in South India, where he became familiar with Tamil language and literature. After returning to England he worked as a chaplain in a psychiatric hospital, and then as a Jungian analyst in private practice. He has written books and papers on theology, analytical psychology and Tamil studies in English and Tamil, including an English translation of the Periya Purāṇam (The History of the Holy Servants of the Lord Siva).